THE SPIRIT of SYNERGY

God's Power and You

L. ROBERT KECK

Abingdon
Nashville

THE SPIRIT OF SYNERGY: GOD'S POWER AND YOU

Library of Congress Cataloging in Publication Data

Keck, L Robert, 1935–
    The spirit of synergy.

    Bibliography: p. 1. Meditation. 2. Keck, L. Robert, 1935-   3.
Methodist Church—Clergy—Biography. 4. Clergy—United States—Biography. 5. Faith-cure. I. Title. BV4813.K42   615'.852 [B]   78-732

ISBN 0-687-39183-0

MANUFACTURED BY THE PARTHENON PRESS AT
NASHVILLE, TENNESSEE, UNITED STATES OF AMERICA

To

LINDSAY
JIM
KRISTA

Contents

Foreword

I have known Bob Keck for many years, including a period of time when we were colleagues on the staff of First Community Church in Columbus, Ohio. I knew him at first as an athlete, an urban pastor deeply involved in social change, a man professionally concerned with education and youth, a middle-American with roots in Iowa Methodism.

In the First Community years I watched the pain grow in Bob's face, as the crippling of which he writes in this book began getting to him. I watched him become impassive in order to hide the pain, stand up in meetings because he couldn't bear to remain seated, withdraw from a meeting in order not to lose composure. I watched his interest in the possibility of religious/psychological healing develop into a passionate search born out of his own suffering.

With admiration I observed Bob pursuing doctors, researchers, and healers of many disciplines and methodologies, open to whatever "worked" regardless of its theoretical orthodoxy. He persuaded Lilly Endowment, First Community Foundation and Church, and many individuals including me to support his research project. I have had opportunity both at First Community and at Kirkridge Retreat and Study Center to observe his workshops and to see the ways in which people touched by his ministry have found insight, healing, and fresh energy for their own spiritual journeys.

So I am pleased to recommend this book as an authentic story of a Christian man who in finding his own healing has also found a healing ministry of significance. The book yields impressive evidence of wide and deep reading in allied fields such as religion, psychology, medicine, into which his research has led. In a popularized field where there is much gold and much more fool's gold, this book provides a sound, knowledgeable, and provocative exploration of what's happening on the spiritual frontiers.

The style of the book is personal, often autobiographical, mixed well with available research and suggested methodologies for personal and corporate meditation. The book will be useful to the individual reader seeking help for his own prayer life, and also of value to the person seeking knowledge and tools to facilitate others on their spiritual journey.

The book is a valuable contribution to the life and work of the church today. I heartily recommend it!

Robert A. Raines
Kirkridge Retreat and Study Center

Preface

This book begins with a description of a personal journey through several years of increasing pain and the search for and discovery of a non-drug relief from that pain. The experiences and insights of that journey profoundly changed my life, both personally and professionally.

Three years of subsequent research and development resulted in refining these experiences and insights into a system of Christian prayer—utilizing the meditative state of consciousness. Several thousand Christians—lay and clergy—participated in experiments and workshops giving evidence that meditative prayer is catalytic to the spiritual lives of many diverse types of people.

The entire experience has been one enormous serendipity for me, and my gratitude for the many who played large and small roles in that process far transcends my ability to express it in words.

My colleagues on the staff of First Community Church and many in that congregation were magnificently supportive and enabling, all the way from the early stages of struggling with the pain to the sharing of the vision that my experience had broader implications. The generosity of that congregation provided the seed funding for that research and continues to provide both hospitable and economic support. It is a unique congregation and I treasure our relationship. During the initial research project a committee comprised of Donna and Don Gepfert, Arlene and Wayne Pipkin, Barbara and Sandy Wood, and Susan and Paul Younger provided very helpful counsel and advice.

I have a particular sense of gratitude for Bob Raines, who as a friend and senior minister of First Community Church when all this began, played a significantly enabling role and who was gracious enough to contribute a foreword for this book.

The Lilly Endowment of Indianapolis, Indiana, and the First Community Foundation and the Patton Foundation, both of Columbus, Ohio, provided the support in terms of money, without which our research could not have covered the scope that it did. I have particular appreciation for Landrum Bolling and John Patton for their generosity of spirit, enthusiastic minds, and visioning capabilities.

The substance and content of meditative prayer, as well as the articulation represented by the manuscript were helped tremendously by the critical reflections of John Cobb, Jr., Joe Deegan, Van Bogard Dunn, James Fenhagen, Joseph Hough, David Lull, Robert Raines, Carolyn Stahl, Sallie TeSelle, Colin Williams, and Barry Woodbridge.

The writing of this manuscript was made considerably more pleasant than it otherwise might have been by the generous sharing of beautiful and stimulating spaces by such friends as Ruby Birge, Elizabeth Davis, Frances Keck (my mother as well as my friend), John Patton, and John and Ann Ross.

There is no way I could adequately identify the many ways that I have benefited these past four years by my colleague

Miriam Clark. Her love, care, and contributions have far surpassed the typing of the manuscript, the helpful suggestions regarding content, and the help in keeping me organized.

My children, Lindsay, Jim, and Krista, to whom this book is dedicated, already have my deepest love. In addition, however, I want to express my gratitude for the depth and tenacity of their love which has survived the many challenges related to the intense pain, and the compromised vacations while I was writing this book. There is both hurt and hurrah in all that, but most of all there is love.

The deepest gratitude in my life, is my new bride of each day, Diane. Her love, deep abiding wisdom, and celebration of every symbol of life provide the sustenance and surprises that keep life solid and serendipitous.

Her gifts are many, and are reflected not only in, but between and behind the lines of this book.

PART I

A PERSONAL JOURNEY INTO A MIRACLE

CHAPTER 1

Dominated by Pain

I was approaching my mid-thirties and those handball tournaments were getting harder every year. But the state championship was next weekend, and I had a title to defend.

A little voice commonly referred to as "my better judgment" said, "Look, dummy, leave that tournament stuff to the younger fellows. Because of polio, you get cramps during a tournament and all during the following night, so your muscles don't have adequate rest and recovery. You've had a broken back, four screws inserted in corrective surgery, and too many birthdays; arthritis and sclerosis have set in. You're in constant pain *without* the tournament stuff and miserable for days *after* a tournament. Stay home!"

"Dummy" muttered something about the doctor saying that it wouldn't do the back any harm to play handball, and besides the fellowship and competition is fun. So I made plans to enter the tournament.

The weekend was complicated by the fact that, in my role as a minister, I had a wedding scheduled at 1:00 P.M. on

Saturday, which, if I got that far in the tournament, would be right between the semifinals and the finals. That might not sound too complicated, until you realize the tournament was 135 miles away.

I couldn't quite bring myself to ask the young couple to postpone their wedding to facilitate my handball tournament, so some careful plans were laid to enable this madness.

It was finally all arranged: I would drive up to the tournament on Friday. If I won the early matches and got through the Saturday morning semifinals with a victory, I would have just enough time to drive back to Des Moines, grab a bit of lunch and get to the church in time for the wedding. Then, following the wedding, Dave Holmes would fly me in his private plane back to Cedar Rapids, arriving just in time to play the finals.

It all went like clockwork. The tournament was over; I had won the championship, and Dave, my good friend Cleo Murphy who had gone along, and I were ready for a leisurely flight back home.

What I had not been paying much attention to, however, were the messages my body was sending me. I had really pushed my body to the limit. The matches had been particularly tough. I had been up most of Friday night with cramping muscles. In spite of eating the usual number of meals, I had sustained a net weight loss of twelve pounds during the twenty-four-hour period from late afternoon on Friday to late afternoon on Saturday. As I got out of the plane at the Des Moines airport, both thighs cramped. I was leaning up against the plane, trying to get the cramps out when I blacked out. I can remember only vaguely Cleo driving his car out to the plane and helping me get home.

I don't remember what happened about the worship service

on Sunday at the small Methodist church I served. For several days I lay in bed with a tremendous amount of pain.

That was the end of State handball tournaments for me! "Dummy" finally listened to his "better judgment."

It was not the end of the pain, unfortunately. In spite of being more moderate in terms of the challenges I gave my body, the pain gradually increased, as did the medication prescribed by my doctors. The medical profession, after much diagnostic work, had said there was nothing more that could be done—except to take stronger drugs. The prognosis was for continued deterioration of my back, greater pain, less flexibility, and the likelihood of being confined to a wheelchair by the time I was forty.

Later that year I joined the staff of First Community Church in Columbus, Ohio. The pain continued to get worse. By late 1972 it was dominating my consciousness and intimidating my life-style. I was out of all forms of athletics I had enjoyed, could stand only for about five minutes at a time, was on a very strong drug for the pain, and had to take a stool into the pulpit to preach.

I was getting desperate. I tried to will the pain away, but that didn't work. I never had been much of a prayer, but I tried to pray the pain away; that didn't work either. (I was aware that it isn't very proper theologically to use prayer as a last-ditch aspirin, but I was in a great deal of pain, and I didn't care whether the theologians thought I was proper or not!)

Then in January of 1973 I had a dream. I was not in the habit of remembering my dreams or of giving them any particular attention. But this one dream came through with extraordinary power. I wrote it down, which was not my custom. Then I promptly forgot about it, which *was* my custom!

Several months later, cleaning out a drawer, I discovered the account of that dream and realized then that it had been a symbolic preview of what had taken place in the intervening months: a fascinating journey through a number of arenas of human discovery, a solution to the severe pain, the discovery of a new concept and practice of prayer which elicited enthusiasm, motivation, and even discipline from a confirmed non-prayer, and a change in direction professionally in order to further research and develop this new approach to Christian prayer.

The dream went something like this: One morning I was sick and decided to stay at home rather than leave for work. I was home alone, and as the day wore on I began to hear voices down in the basement. Eventually I went to investigate and discovered there was an office in my basement and a man working there. From the equipment in the room and the drawings that were around, it was obvious the man was an architect. As I conversed with him, he revealed to me that he was the architect of *my* home.

I exclaimed that not only was I surprised that he was the designer of my home but that I had been totally unaware of his office being there! It struck me as incredible that I had been oblivious to the fact that someone had an office in my basement!

The architect told me that there was something else to which I had been oblivious: There were more rooms in my home than I had explored. He began giving me a tour. He opened door after door, showing me rooms I had not known were there. The most striking thing I remember about the rooms is that there were no walls—no boundaries, no limits! The next day, instead of going back to work, I began showing some of my friends the rooms the architect had shown me and trying to share my enthusiasm for what a fascinating home it was. That was the end of the dream.

What I now believe is that the home was symbolic of me, the

design known as Bob Keck, that I was to meet in a fresh way the Architect (God), the Designer of this space, and that God had created many more rooms in this house than I was aware of—rooms without limits. "In my Father's house are many rooms" (John 14:2).

What happened in real life was that during the succeeding few months, the "Architect" actually gave me a tour of some of those "rooms"—the untapped resources in the human design. I must tell you frankly, though, that during the time of my touring I had no inkling that what I was doing would lead to anything having to do with prayer. I was simply, and rather single-mindedly, looking for some relief from pain. Nevertheless, just as the dream predicted, I became so impressed with the new space the architect had showed me—and its implications for the Christian life—that I did indeed eventually change directions professionally.

CHAPTER 2

A Tour
by the Architect

FAITH HEALING

The first "room" I checked out was faith healing, or spiritual healing. After all, I was a minister, wasn't I? I was supposed to be a professional in this faith business, so if faith could heal—why not *me*?

Of course, as we all know, my professional training to be a clergyman did not train me *in* faith; it trained me to intellectualize *about* faith, to know about the history of faith and the church, and to be able to study the Bible in a scholarly way. Besides, sophisticated Christians are supposed to be skeptical about faith healing—aren't we? Nevertheless, if would take away that pain, I was willing to be unsophisticated!

It didn't work—not for me at that time in my life. I couldn't set my intellect aside, and I had too much difficulty with the theology I encountered. The notion that God would perform miracles, that is, break with the natural laws of the universe on command from someone using the right words—I couldn't buy that. I could not believe that God was so parochial as to shed favors upon those who believed in a certain prescribed way; nor could I believe that we could manipulate God by using the right words. I also, at that time, had difficulty with the faith healers' reluctance to explain what was at work. "Just believe," they would say to me. I had difficulty with that because my notion of our relationship with God does not rule out intellectual or rational understanding.

In all fairness, I should say that since this early exposure to faith healing, I have encountered others who approach it more sensibly. I now see a larger picture within which I can take a different view toward faith healing. It is clear that there is such a profound interrelationship of body, mind, and spirit, as well as so much power in one's belief structure, that it now seems to me terribly naive to say that faith healing is impossible. We will get into those matters later. The fact is that at that particular time in my journey, my skepticism was not satisfied in the faith healing "room." So I left, still in pain, and the Architect took me to the next room.

PSYCHIC HEALING

This room was labeled "psychic healing." Again it was with a great deal of skepticism that I entered. Consequently, I entered only intellectually, not through an experiential encounter. This, no doubt, is the main reason why I again failed to find a solution to my pain. Nevertheless, this room was not without its impact upon me and, in fact, played a significant role in preparing me for what was to come later.

The difficulty with much psychic healing is that its evidence is primarily anecdotal. You can listen endlessly to fascinating stories, but that does not convince a skeptic or make actual healing possible. Two dramatic psychic healers did catch my attention. They were the focus of a great amount of testing and research. One was Edgar Cayce, a humble photographer who lived from 1877 to 1945 in the United States. Cayce, who had no formal medical training, discovered he could go into a trance and diagnose people's illnesses—even at great distances and without knowing them. He would then prescribe unconventional remedies. The amazing thing about Cayce's work is that in spite of literally thousands of carefully kept records, many enthusiastic followers, and even a medical clinic's experimenting with the interface between modern medicine and the Cayce "readings," conventional medical theorists seem hardly to have ventured a glance at him.[1]

Another incredible story is that of the Brazilian peasant Arigó (1918-1971).[2] Arigó had completed only four years of schooling and had worked as a farmhand, a miner, and had operated a small café. No evidence of extraordinary gifts was present until he was thirty-two. One day in 1950 Arigó was staying in a small hotel in the state capital, Belo Horizonte. A state senator by the name of Bittencourt was in the same hotel. Bittencourt, who had been diagnosed by his doctors as having an inoperable lung tumor, says that Arigó entered his room at 2:00 A.M. and told him to lie down on the bed. To Bittencourt's amazement, Arigó pulled out a straight razor and proceeded to operate on his chest, removing the tumor.

Bittencourt could hardly believe what was happening. He must be dreaming! Yet his pajamas were torn and a baseball-sized tumor was there on the bedstand. There was blood on his pajamas but no scar. In a subsequent examination by his doctor, it was confirmed: *the tumor had disappeared.*

What's going on here? That kind of thing is not supposed to happen. Modern medicine knows that can't happen! Maybe stories get exaggerated over a period of time. Miracles have

A *Tour by the Architect*

supposedly been performed by Jesus and other saints, but Arigó? If Arigó was a saint, the church has not been informed about it.

Fortunately, Arigó was still alive and still performing these "impossible" surgical operations when word of him reached the United States. In 1968, the renowned Dr. Henry Puharich, a physician who had spent many years in medical electronics research and who holds more than sixty United States and foreign patents, led a team of six doctors and eight paramedical specialists to Brazil to study Arigó. Dr. Puharich and his colleagues watched Arigó performing surgery without anesthesia or any normal sterilization and confirmed that his patients had no postoperative complications. Dr. Puharich was dumbfounded and later wrote:

It was truly a mind-shattering experience to see every principle of surgery violated with impunity. Indeed, I found myself unable to accept the data of my own senses.

In order to overcome this mental blockage, I decided that I must personally experience what Arigó's patients were experiencing during surgery. If such an experience could be obtained, I felt, it might clear my shocked belief system and perceptions. Arigó agreed to operate on a lipoma (benign tumor) on my right elbow. The operation scene was a room in which some ninety people crowded around Arigó to see him operate. Arigó with a flourish requested that someone furnish him with a pocket knife, and someone in the audience produced one. Arigó took hold of my right wrist with his left hand and wielded the borrowed pocket knife with his right hand. I was told not to watch the operation on my arm, so I turned my head toward my cameraman and directed the motion-picture work. The next thing I knew was that Arigó had placed a tumor and the knife in my hand. In spite of being perfectly conscious I had not felt any pain. In fact, I had no sensation at all at the surgical site. I was sure that I had not been hypnotized. Yet there was the incision in my arm, which was bleeding, and there was the tumor from my arm. Subsequent analysis of the film showed that the entire operation lasted five seconds. Arigó had made two strokes with the knife on the skin. The skin had split wide open, and the tumor was clearly visible. Arigó then squeezed the tumor as one might squeeze a boil, and the tumor popped out.

I felt that I had been hoodwinked, because I had experienced nothing. However, knowing that the knife was dirty, that my skin was not cleansed, and that Arigó's hands were not clean, there was a good chance of getting an infection, perhaps even blood poisoning. I felt that if this would heal without infection, then I could believe that Arigó had an influence on the healing process. If it got infected or blood poisoning set in, I felt I could always be flown to a hospital in Rio de Janeiro and be saved by modern medicine. Therefore, I covered the wound with a band aid, which I removed every twenty-four hours in order to photograph the wound. The result of this experiment was that the wound healed clean (without a drop of pus) within three days, about half the time required normally.[3]

Arigó was killed in an accident in 1971. However, since Arigó was the subject of careful study and observation by a team of physicians as recently as 1968, I will use Arigó's work to illustrate several extraordinary principles which are demonstrated by numerous psychic healers.

While in the psychic healing "room," I was impressed by five observations: (1) blatant challenges to the best of modern medical theory, (2) the frequent use of an altered state of consciousness, (3) a holistic approach to healing, (4) the idea that pain is not an objective phenomenon, and (5) the element of mystery.

First of all, psychic healing challenges conventional medical knowledge. Arigó never used anesthetics, yet his patients never complained of pain. He never used any process of sterilization, yet nobody suffered from any form of infection. He made consistently accurate diagnoses, even using conventional medical terminology, yet he had never had any medical training. Arigó never used any of the equipment that modern medicine uses for diagnosis; he simply would look at the patient for a few seconds and then offer his diagnosis. Also, Arigó's patients were healed at a rate far surpassing our expectations. No stitches were used by Arigó to close a wound, and yet no scars remained.

Second, an altered state of consciousness was involved in the healing process. According to Dr. Puharich, Arigó did not seem to be in a trance state, as Cayce was, but he claimed to be receiving all his instructions from a voice speaking into his ear. Arigó said the voice was that of a deceased German medical student, Adolphus Fritz.

Third, psychic healing seems to be more holistic than our conventional approach to medical care. For instance, the conventional physician would usually treat a stomach ulcer with a diet, an antacid, and possibly a tranquilizer. Arigó, however, would not focus upon the stomach at all. He would look throughout the body/mind/spirit unity of the person for all the problems that eventually were expressed in the stomach with an ulcer. He seemed to be operating on the notion that if all parts of the person were functioning properly, the ulcer would heal rapidly (and not reoccur).

Fourth, pain is not an objectively perceived phenomenon. Arigó could perform a delicate eye operation with a knife without causing the patient any pain, yet no anesthetic was used. Dr. Puharich and his colleagues witnessed hundreds of such operations. At the least, this points to the phenomenon of pain as being something other than a given. Pain evidently does not *have* to be!

And fifth, much of psychic healing is simply mysterious. We

cannot make sense out of it. Many of the mind-boggling aspects of Arigó's work we have already touched upon. There is one other fact, however, that is still more confounding. In his more than twenty years of healing, Arigó was never able to heal himself or members of his family! Why, no one knows. Arigó explained that it was not he but "Dr. Fritz" who was the healer, and he himself could not affect this paradoxical situation.

ACUPUNCTURE

By the time I reached the room designated "acupuncture," I was becoming so fascinated with the enormous potential that God has created within the human being—potential that most of us allow to lie dormant—that I was gaining hope that there might be a "natural" way of dealing with pain. Consequently, I decided to bypass what appeared to be a system dependent upon a physician using needles and continue my search for a self-sufficient method of pain management.

However, I ventured into this room just long enough to become interested in the concept of energy upon which acupuncture is based. The theory is that energy moves throughout the meridians or pathways of the body in two forms, *yin* and *yang*. When there is an equal balance of yin and yang, healthy conditions exist. Imbalance produces pathology. The way to health is to restore the balanced flow of energy.

There are many means for restoring the flow: chemicals, massage, electrified needles, Laser beams, and even what William Tiller (a physicist and chairman of the department of materials science at Stanford University) calls the undisputed best method—"spiritual energy injection."

In fact, this notion of energy flow throughout the body which comes from the Eastern philosophies is being confirmed by Western scientists. Tiller and Victor Adamenko, a Russian physicist, have independently discovered that acupuncture points can be detected with a simple instrument called a Wheatstone bridge, which measures electrical resistance. There is a 95 percent drop in electrical resistance of the skin at acupuncture points compared to other areas of the body.

When we compare the possibilities for use of metaphysical energy emerging from ancient and modern insights on the subject with the way we currently conceive of and use energy, we may confront a serious question about Christian stewardship of our potential. We may face a significant "energy crisis," if you will. Consider: Throughout history many cultures have been interested enough in metaphysical energy to have special words for it. The ancient Egyptians called it *ka*. The Hindus and yogis call it *prana*. The Hawaiians call it *mana*. The Russian researchers call it *bioplasma*. And the Chinese call it *ch'i*. We in the West, preoccupied with a pre-Einsteinian notion of matter, have simply ignored metaphysical energy.

Another area of research that raises some question marks about energy is Kirlian photography. This is a lensless electrical photographic process, named after its developers, two Russian scientists, S. D. and K. Kirlian. The process was introduced in 1939, and since that time, it has raised more questions than it has answered. It seems to be recording an aura surrounding the body, some kind of usually invisible energy emanating from the body. The "energy" photographed changes according to one's mental and physical condition. If one is relaxed and in good physical condition, the corona tends to be pale to dark blue in color. If a person is in a state of arousal, the corona is typically red and white.

Is it possible that this energy emission is the same aura some people are able to see, and could this explain why Jesus and many of the saints and mystics of the past were depicted with halos? Could it also be that this energy can be transferred from person to person? Is this what happens in the "laying on of hands," long a method of healing in Christianity? Research has shown a distinct change in the corona of a healer's fingertips depending on whether or not the mind is directed toward healing.

Sister Justa Smith, a Franciscan nun who holds a doctorate in biochemistry and is research director of the Human Dimensions Institute in Buffalo, New York, has analyzed several healers. Her study is centered around the enzyme trypsin, which is produced by the pancreas and is essential to the body's ability to combat disease. Dr. Smith has used the enzyme trypsin as the object to be affected in her experiments with healers so as to eliminate the possible psychological factors in human subjects. She has discovered that the laying on of hands has the same affect on the enzymes as a highly magnetic field. This result raises the question, Is spiritual energy magnetic in nature? Magnetism has also been demonstrated to facilitate healing in broken bones, and some of today's cancer research is exploring the efficacy of magnetic involvement in the treatment of aberrant cells.

In totally separate research by the institute for Bioenergetic Analysis in New York, the energy field around the body was found to be affected by the rhythm of breathing. Could there be a correlation between this modern scientific finding and the yogic notion of *prana,* the energy that a person taps into with breathing exercises? And what about the fact that the Hebrew words for *spirit, wind,* and *breath,* so closely related to one another in the Bible, come from the same root?

More and more, our questions become relevant to one another, and our curiosity stirs up even deeper puzzles as the facts emerge. Biofeedback research done with electroencephalogram (EEG), electromyograph (EMG), and electrocardiogram (EKG) equipment reveal that the muscles and organs of the body give off electrical energy. Psychokenesis, the ability to move objects without touching them physically and without using other devices, seems to indicate the possible transfer of energy from the human mind/body onto a separate object. Quantum physics claims that all matter is energy. Aikido, an Oriental martial art, is based upon energy awareness. Kundalini is a Yoga discipline based on the idea that energy travels up the spine.

Our culture has tended to trust what it could see. We cannot see energy, only the results of it. Of course, the same thing is true of love, which is perhaps the most powerful form of energy. Perhaps this is reason enough to keep looking for the question marks. Our continued curiosity and research may bring us to a better understanding and use of the metaphysical energy that God is, and is creating.

In the acupuncture "room" I had been introduced to exciting concepts of energy. It was all very fascinating; and I had no doubt that there were very important implications for our total understanding of the human being there. Nevertheless, I was still in excruciating pain and I had to find some relief.

By this time I was convinced that the Architect had created within this house a room or combination of rooms that would hold an answer to enable me to deal with this pain without either taking drugs or making perpetual visits to the doctor's office. So I asked the Architect to continue the tour.

BIOFEEDBACK

The next room I came to was labeled "biofeedback." The roots of biofeedback go back to the turn of the century when a fellow by the name of Oskar Vogt discovered that people could, by themselves, use the principles of hypnosis. After all, the "bottom line" in hypnosis is the power of one's own imagination.

In the 1920s a German, J. H. Schultz, developed what was called autogenic training, which used the power of one's imagination to affect one's physiology. And in just the past two decades, American researchers like Elmer Green, Joe Kamiya, Barbara Brown, Tom Budzynski, and Neal Miller have brought electronics into this picture to develop what has become known as biofeedback training.

A biofeedback machine is simply any electronic device that monitors what is going on inside your body and gives you instantaneous audible or visual feedback so you can see or hear what is happening. Just as a thermometer reacts to body temperature and records it, a biofeedback machine records whatever it is monitoring (brain waves, blood flow, blood pressure, heartbeat, or any other internal function) and almost simultaneously transmits that information to you.

Biofeedback *training* is simply the process by which you learn to control that particular system which is being monitored. The basic principle at work is this: The mind and body are so profoundly linked that the normal person can, with the split-second monitoring information available, learn to control the body in ways previously considered impossible.

This process of learning is really very familiar to us. We learn how to pick up a fork off the dinner table by first getting visual feedback—we see where it is. Then we get tactile feedback—we feel the fork when we touch it. And we have learned to use the muscles of our hand and arm to pick up the fork through experimentation—trial and error. So it is with biofeedback. Say I am hooked up to an EMG (electromyograph), which measures muscle tension. A tone system provides the feedback. If the tone is relatively high, it tells me there is a lot of tension in my muscles. I imagine that I am lying on a beautiful beach in northern Wisconsin: the tone goes down, indicating to me that there is less tension in my muscles. Or I imagine I am going to play handball with Bill Reichardt (he's good!): tension—the tone goes up. What I am learning is that my thoughts have a direct correlation with the tension level in my muscles. Likewise, in biofeedback training we can learn to control our blood flow, which has important implications for anyone suffering from migraine headaches or Raynaud's disease, both of which are manifested as blood flow problems.

Biofeedback research and training are just in their infancy. Consequently, no one knows for sure what the long-range impact will be. Nevertheless, I get a feeling of importance to this "room." And again, several observations stand out. First of all, biofeedback is another powerful testimony to a linkage between mind and body far surpassing our previous belief. Since our senses give us feedback primarily on external data, we have assumed that many of the internal systems were beyond our control.

Hindu yogis have been saying for centuries that in a meditative state of consciousness they could control physiological systems previously thought to be impossible to control. Our culture has paid little attention either medically or spiritually. Now, however, our machines are sending us that same message, and we listen. It is a telling commentary that we will listen to machines when we would not listen to holy men from another culture. Be that as it may, it is for this very reason that I suspect biofeedback will be the most effective bridge, for our culture, between the old belief structure that separated mind and body and the emerging new belief structure that recognizes the intimate linkage.

Traditionally, technology has seemed to deny the power of

subjectivity—the world of emotion, thought, feeling, and intuition. Now we find our biofeedback machines confirming both the reality and the power of subjectivity.

The second outstanding observation was that the power of the mind-body linkage was released through deep relaxation and the use of imagery. I will expand on this in chapter 12.

And finally, I consistently found biofeedback researchers coming to the edge and frequently into the realm of mysticism and not having a vocabulary adequate to explain the phenomena. Dr. Barbara Brown, one of the earliest and foremost of biofeedback researchers says, "Obviously, the new horizons of mind revealed to an expanded awareness will be known only when awareness takes us there. . . . We resort to the models of mysticism of an earlier age to describe our moments of altered states of consciousness. We use words like supraconsciousness, hallucinatory, metaphysical, intangibles, or other world."[4]

Just as I was becoming fascinated with biofeedback and was wanting to explore it more deeply for its possible help in alleviating pain, the phone rang. It was my doctor, Ernie Johnson, a brilliant specialist in physical medicine who had guided the most recent diagnostic work on my back problems. "How would you like to try hypnosis?" Dr. Johnson inquired. "I've got this friend out in Utah, a physician who trains other physicians in the technique of medical hypnosis. He has agreed to teach you self-hypnosis in order to deal with your back pain. Incidentally, years ago he taught self-hypnosis to Roy Burkhart, then senior minister at First Community Church and he is intrigued that you are also a minister and at the same church."

Hypnosis? I thought that was occult stuff. And yet Dr. Johnson was recommending that I look into it? And Roy Burkhart was taught by the same Dr. Baer? I turned to the

Architect. Is there a room in this house labeled "medical hypnosis"? Sure enough, he said there was—right across the hall. I left the biofeedback room, knowing that I would be back. But now I had a lot of reading to do in preparation for my trip to see Dr. Baer.

MEDICAL HYPNOSIS

I hustled over to the room labeled "medical hypnosis." It was not without some fear and trepidation, however—what with images of a hypnotist making a fool out of me. I figured that *I* made a fool out of myself plenty of times, and I didn't need anybody's help in doing *that!*

Nevertheless, I was miserable with the pain; I didn't like what the drugs were doing with my head; I hated my pain for being the center of attention every time I was with somebody; and I had a lot of respect for Dr. Johnson. So, why not?

As soon as I entered the medical hypnosis room, I immediately went to the bookshelves to read about the subject. (I'm more courageous intellectually than I am in some other ways.) It was a real revelation! When I got into the literature regarding the good, substantive research in clinical and experimental hypnosis, it proved about 90 percent of what I *had* believed about the subject to be false. Hypnosis does not mean letting somebody else have control over one's mind. I would simply decide to let the doctor guide me in a process that maximizes the use of my own imagination. Hypnosis is not a trance, nor is one asleep. The term *hypnosis* literally means "sleep" and is therefore a misnomer. Actually, hypnosis is a state of increased awareness facilitated by the concentration of the deeply relaxed state of mind.

Besides realizing that I had held many false assumptions regarding hypnosis, I began to see a deep underlying similarity with some of the other disciplines I had been studying—the linkage of mind and body facilitated by the power of our imagination in a deeply relaxed state. The roots of hypnosis go back to the eighteenth-century physician, Franz Anton Mesmer, from whom we get our word "mesmerized." Although Mesmer called his technique "animal magnetism," a Royal Commission appointed by Louis XVI (which, incidentally, included Ben Franklin) investigated it and concluded that magnetism had nothing to do with it. *The power,* the commission concluded, *was in the person's own imagination.* Further research into hypnosis revealed that persons responded according to their belief—their image—of how one was *supposed* to respond. Dr. Ainslie Meares, a past president of the International Society for Clinical and Experimental Hypnosis says, "The patient's behavior in hypnosis is largely governed by his preconceived ideas as to how a person does behave when hypnotized."[5]

My hesitation about trying hypnosis vanished when I learned I would not be unconscious. On the contrary, I would be aware of what was happening and could stop it at any time. So I got on the plane and headed for Salt Lake City.

No sooner had I met Dr. Baer than he started throwing ski equipment in his van and talking about skiing. "But—I don't know how to ski," I said.

"I'll teach you," Dr. Baer replied.

"But—I have this bad back," I weakly retorted.

"Well," said Dr. Baer with a smile on his face and a twinkle in his eye, "if you break your leg, it'll make you forget about your back!"

What kind of doctor is this, I thought, a sadist? What have I got myself into? He *seems* to be a nice guy, he's a friend of Dr. Johnson's, he has a very nice wife and family, he even took me to hear the Mormon Tabernacle Choir. He *must* be all right. Anyhow, I'd love to learn how to ski!

A Tour by the Architect

The first day Dr. Baer began teaching me the techniques of hypnosis, going through the process of deep relaxation and focusing of my imagination. I tried to imagine that I was breathing away the pain with each breath. *Nothing!* I didn't make a dent in the pain. I would have taken a little time to be depressed, but Dr. Baer didn't give me a chance. We were out on the slopes—with ski equipment on. How did I get here? Did he hypnotize me to get me out here? No, I was awake throughout the whole session. Five minutes of trying to ski and—*Wow!* Did my back hurt!

Dr. Baer knew just how to get to me. "This is the *Bunny Hill,*" he said with emphasis. "Aren't you ever going to learn how to ski this little hill?" Okay, that did it. I was back on my feet trying to master the beginner's hill. A few more trips down that little slope and the pain again. It *really* hurt now, in spite of my medication.

I started to complain to the good doctor, and before I knew it we were on a gondola heading for the top of the mountain. I then discovered a new way to be oblivious to pain—*fear!*

Fear also blocks out memory—I don't know how I got down that mountain!

That night the options were clear: (1) I was going to get some success from this hypnosis training, or (2) I was going to suffer great pain, or (3) I was going to die of fear. I wasn't sure about the first, was already experiencing the second, and figured the chances were very good for the third.

There was intensive work on the techniques of hypnosis for the next several days—in between skiing, of course. We worked on relaxation. We worked on concentration. We worked on imagining—as clearly and powerfully as I could—that each exhalation would flush out the pain from my body. Then a miracle happened—the pain was gone. Dr. Baer was the *bearer* (pun intended) of a miracle!

What is this—Keck, a liberal who has always tried to demythologize miracles, talking about a real miracle? Yes, real; the pain was really diminished—about 80 percent gone. Would it last or was it just temporary? Maybe the skiing and the gondola ride just scared it away? I set aside the medication but not too far. The pain might come back.

Whatever the long-range results, I knew something important had happened, and my heart felt an enormous gratitude to God for the many beautiful gifts in this miracle. That night, when all the rest were in bed, I sat looking at the single rose that my friends in Columbus had sent. It has long been a tradition at First Community Church to give a single red rose at important moments in someone's life. How could they have known *how* important this time would be for me? The rose stood on the table magnificently silhouetted against the large glass window, beyond which towered the fantastic ski slopes of Park City illumined by the full moon. A sight of such beauty I have seldom experienced. And you know, it's even more beautiful with tears in your eyes and a prayer of thanksgiving in your heart.

CHAPTER 3

Understanding a Miracle: The Why and How of Pain Relief

Miracles do not happen in contradiction to nature, but only in contradiction to that which is known to us about nature.
                                                        —Augustine

That miracle was not just temporary. It has lasted to this day. Of course, I continue a daily process—which I call meditative prayer but which is a synthesis of the insights learned from all the "rooms" in the Architect's tour. It's been five years now without having to experience the majority of that pain; I need no pain-killing drugs; and I'm back on the handball and tennis courts! I've also passed my fortieth birthday and am nowhere close to being confined to a wheelchair. Yet, the effects of polio are still present, and the screws are still in my back as a result of the earlier surgery. A miracle, indeed!

Once the miracle had come about, it seemed to me that it would be all right to try to understand it. I seriously doubt that God is offended if we attempt to make sense out of what happens to us. Frequently I find I do not understand something until long after I have experienced it. (This tardy intellect is probably no surprise to some of my teachers of years past.) Actually, I think the reason for this is that a profound experience involves much more than the intellect. Because this kind of experience involves the whole being, it is only after intellect has the opportunity to reflect on all the various aspects that its significance becomes apparent.

Although this miracle came about with apparent suddenness, it was, in fact, the result of gathering insights and perceptions coming together in a momentary Gestalt, a *whole* experience involving my body, mind, and spirit that created a breakthrough in my control over pain. As I looked back over the previous ten years of living with that pain and at my "tour by the Architect," I could begin to dissect and understand that miraculous Gestalt.

First of all, I realized that not only had conventional medical science "struck out" in terms of getting rid of my own pain but that the situation for all chronic pain patients was generally discouraging. In the United States alone, according to an April, 1977, *Newsweek* article on pain, people like myself are spending $10 billion a year on prescription drugs and surgery for pain, with an additional $900 million being spent for over-the-counter pills and salves. The average chronic pain patient has suffered for seven years, had three to five operations, and has a 50 percent chance of having acquired a drug habit. Obviously I was not the only one who needed a better solution to pain. Conventional pain management simply did not have a very good record! This realization led me to question our basic assumptions about pain and the conventional management of pain. For instance:

Understanding a Miracle

A. I used to think pain was a message that something was wrong physically—period. Now I know that pain is usually *holistic*, involving *body*, *mind*, and *spirit* messages. The doctors had diagnosed my pain as being the result of polio, which left my muscles with a high propensity for cramps and spasms, and of the broken back, the screws, and resultant arthritis and sclerosis in the spine. If I was to get rid of chronic pain, I needed to "hear" all the messages. The physical messages, yes, but also the psychological and spiritual messages. What was the pain telling me about excessive stress in my life? Or more precisely, my *reaction* to the stress in my life. And what was the pain telling me about the large spiritual issues of my life, namely, meaning and purpose in my life?

My policy was and is that if one is sitting on a tack, it's better to "hear" the message and get up than to take some drugs so that it doesn't hurt so much. To hear all the messages coming to me in my pain, therefore, I needed to carefully examine every aspect of my life: my job, my marriage, the way I was relating to my family and to others, my self-image, my hopes, my fears, my total theology and psychology, as well as my physiology. Where were the stresses, the strains, the imbalances? I became convinced that liberation from the pain had to start with facing up to the messages coming from within the pain.

B. I used to think pain was an objective given and that the only factor that caused people to experience pain differently was a "pain threshold." Some people evidently had high thresholds and some, low thresholds. Now I know that although there is an objective element in pain, most of it is *subjective*. I have major *responsibility for the way I experience pain,* and, most important, *I can affect the experience of pain.* There are several specific factors affecting our experience of pain over which we have some control.

1) We consciously or unconsciously choose pain-related behavior that intensifies or prolongs the experience of pain: the subtle solicitation and acceptance of sympathy, the ways we let pain affect our social situations, our jobs, our marriages, our activity, our total life-style. The way we act to let others know we are in pain is a learned pattern and one developed because of the reinforcement we get: the affection of a spouse when pain occurs, the sympathy of friends or the attention of the doctor, all can affect how and when to show and feel pain.

The point is that we can decide how to react to pain and thereby reduce our experience of pain. There is much more power of choice and self-determination in this experience than we have been led to believe.

2) Our belief structure affects how we experience pain. To some extent we feel pain when and to the degree that we *expect* to feel pain.

Dr. Wilbert Fordyce, professor of psychology at the University of Washington Medical School has described what he calls metric pain. In experiments with chronic pain patients, Dr. Fordyce had the patients go through certain exercises but told them to stop whenever it started to hurt. Observers counted and numbered the repetitions. Eighty percent of the patients stopped the exercises, indicating that they had become painful, on a repetition whose number had a final digit ending in 0 or 5. In other words, four out of five stopped the exercises when the number reached 10 or 15 or 20, et cetera. Only 20 percent stopped on all the other digits combined. If pain were an objective phenomenon, there would have been a random dispersal across all ten final digits. This illustrates again the point that pain is something we choose to experience as far as when and how much. Consequently we also can choose not to experience it!

3) Our state of consciousness affects our experience of pain. In an emergency or in an athletic event, a person may sustain an injury and not even be aware of it until afterward, when consciousness returns to an ordinary state. Likewise, several unusual persons who have been tested in the Menninger Foundation laboratories for exceptional pain control have been found to be using an altered state of consciousness when oblivious to pain.

In many of the rooms I toured with the Architect I saw people demonstrate control over states of consciousness. It follows that learning to alter states of consciousness is another way the pain patient can take control over the experience of pain.

C. I used to think that there were only two ways of getting rid of pain: drugs and surgery. The vested interests of drug companies condition our attitudes through commercials and advertisements. Much of the medical profession similarly influence us. But I in no way want to demean the value of the best in medical diagnosis and the appropriate use of drugs and surgery. I simply want to relate that I have discovered there are many courses one can pursue as an active determinant in one's own health before resorting to the more drastic measures. It is even possible that these more "natural" means of pain relief can be so thorough and successful as to *eliminate any necessity for drugs or surgery.*

For instance, after hearing the messages in the pain, one can—

1) *Make necessary life-style changes.* If the messages say

the musculature of the body is out of shape and not adequately supportive, an exercise program will help. If the messages indicate an excess of stress, perhaps some decisions can be made regarding the major causes of the stress. One can choose to change pain-oriented behavior and to have emotional needs met in better ways.

2) *Develop techniques of stress management.* There are a variety of techniques one can learn to better manage the stress of life: exercise and relaxation methods such as autogenic training, biofeedback training, yoga, transcendental meditation, or meditative prayer.

3) *Use imagery to change the experience of pain.* The use of imagery in an altered state of consciousness is a powerful tool in the management of pain. Biofeedback training, hypnosis, and meditative prayer are systems that could be used for relief of pain.

4) *Learn about medical modalities.* If the above approaches to pain management have been tried thoroughly and conscientiously and the pain is still a major challenge, it may be that further professional help is needed in hearing some messages that have not as yet been heard or that medical assistance with acupuncture, electrical stimulation, acupressure, drugs, or surgery is required. Fortunately, there are now more medical pain clinics making use of the natural mechanisms for pain management before resorting to drugs or surgery.[1]

The miracle of pain relief happened for me because of the "tour by the Architect," hearing some important messages about the stresses and strains in my body/mind/spirit, making some life-style changes, and making use of imagery in an altered state of consciousness.

The training from Dr. Baer in the use of imagery came

under the label and with the vocabulary of medical hypnosis. But I soon discovered that hypnosis has no corner on the power of imagery. I now use what I call meditative prayer for a more holistic approach to using imagery. It is this approach that I will describe in detail in Part III.

PART II

AN EMERGING NEW IMAGE OF THE HUMAN BEING

CHAPTER 4

Serendipity!

Well now, since that bothersome pain problem was taken care of, I could go back to ministry as usual, right? Wrong!

That encounter with the Architect was something more than a casual dream. The Architect was indeed my Creator and the fellowship with the Architect had a meaning all its own. I was a different person, now—in more ways than simply being free of pain.

The tour of the rooms was an experience that profoundly changed me. It was more than an intellectual pilgrimage. God seemed to be nudging me in new directions and calling on me to respond. I was fascinated to find that God was introducing me to areas in which no one has yet discovered the "walls," or limits. I had the distinct feeling that God had led me only to the rooms I was ready for and that there were other rooms to be discovered later. I'm not at all sure that it was a case of my choosing to change directions professionally. It seems, rather, more accurate to say I simply responded to God's initiative. In any case, it is an exciting journey.

Spirit of Synergy: God's Power and You

There is a Persian fairy tale about the three Princes of Serendip. It seems that the three Princes were frequently taking journeys and unexpectedly stumbling across something very valuable. Sir Horace Walpole in 1754 reflected upon this propensity for finding valuable things unexpectedly and coined the word *serendipity*. I had started a journey simply—and rather single-mindedly—to find a nondrug solution to the intense pain I was experiencing. I can only describe what happened, however, an an experience of tremendous serendipity. On this journey I stumbled onto some very exciting insights about the human being—insights that added up to a much larger, more magnificent image of the human being.

Perhaps you, like me, have felt there is some truth in the claim that we are using only a small percentage of our physical, mental, and spiritual abilities. William James, the Harvard psychologist, around the turn of the century, said it more poetically: "Our fires are damped, our drafts are checked, we are living on only a small percentage of our abilities."

My journey made me realize that it might be my small image of human nature that led me to refer to certain people as "exceptional" and assign certain things I didn't understand to the "occult." (Occult, by the way, literally means "hidden.") I began to become aware of how our current popular picture of the human being is limited in the understanding of what constitutes health and disease and of the process leading from the latter to the former. We dismiss miracles like "spontaneous remission" of disease without learning what natural mechanisms of God's creation are at work. Within the larger image of human life that God is now revealing perhaps we will learn how to participate actively in such re-creation of health.

I also saw that I used to call a lot of things *coincidence!*

Serendipity!

I directed a "Y" camp some years ago. Once I awoke in the middle of the night feeling that something was wrong. Ten minutes later the phone rang: one of our canoe trips was in trouble—*coincidence.* While preaching a sermon one day I developed a toothache (I hope no one psychoanalyzes *that* one). I didn't mention anything about it, but after the worship service my friend Carrie came up to me and said she hoped my tooth got better. How did she know? She said she could see a break in my aura. Must just be *coincidence.* There were many occurrences in my life that I had labeled coincidence, until I read Arthur Koestler's *The Roots of Coincidence.* I also discovered that the great psychological scientist Carl Jung didn't believe in coincidence either. Another of my assumptions would clearly need to be reevaluated.

At first I thought that perhaps my experience in touring the rooms was a serendipity meant only for me personally—a revelation of God only for me. It was clear that many others past and present already accepted a larger image of the human being. Jesus, for instance, evidently had such a harmonious orchestration of body, mind, and spirit that he was capable of many miracles, healing and otherwise. Yet he made the bold statement in John 14:12 that we might be able to do even greater things. Many were far ahead of me in understanding the nature of God's creation, but I knew that there are others who shared with me the limited concept of the human being articulated by the current medical, psychological, spiritual, and social orthodoxy.

What convinced me that God is revealing an enlarged image of the human being for our whole culture was that the insights, which represent only the peaks of the emerging mountain range, began appearing in many different respectable disciplines. It is not *coincidental* that we find emerging at about the same time transpersonal psychology, biofeedback, transpersonal education, authentic psychic research, metapsychiatry, the "Tao of physics," dream research, the holistic health movement, and the presence of Eastern meditative disciplines in the West. God is dropping seeds of revelation (and revolution) all over the place so that growth will be inevitable. Some of us may prove to be very "rocky ground" and not receptive, but certainly not all of us! To be more specific, not only "exceptional" people, but every one of us will be *able to:*

1. Play a much more significant role in our state of health or illness by:
   a. avoiding a larger number of stress-related illnesses (and current research is making that list longer and longer) with deep relaxation and imagery;
   b. aborting migraine headaches or controlling Raynaud's disease by altering blood flow;
   c. aborting the perception of pain without the use of drugs;
   d. substantially affecting high blood pressure, cancer, arthritis, and many other diseases;
   e. being able to harmonize body, mind, and spirit so as to maintain a state of health.

2. Add to the breadth and depth of our life, in addition to being in a state of good health, by:
   a. realizing increased concentration and all the many benefits that are a derivative of better control over attention;
   b. regularly experiencing telepathy, clairvoyance, and precognition;
   c. being able to control weight, smoking, and fears and phobias which now diminish our enjoyment of life

(controlling all these is possible as we get more familiar
with our unconscious);
   d. experiencing the unity of the universe which is God and
      the joy and peace which are the results;
   e. experiencing a sense of personal communion with God.

3. Find a new perception of our relationship with the other
   people who are aboard this "spaceship earth," resulting in
   experiences such as:
   a. a form of communication that is not dependent upon our
      usual means and is not affected by distance (you can call
      it telepathy or intercessory prayer);
   b. a sense of unity that will make possible a greater degree
      of the Christian love ethic. The new image of the human
      being is one that implies profound relationship with all
      the rest of God's creation, through breaking down the
      damnable emphasis upon sovereignty which is at the
      root of so much suffering and social injustice.

Hold on, you may be thinking. I know all this sounds
incredible and utopian. And you may be thinking those screws
are someplace other than in my back. It blew my mind, too,
when I first looked at it, but I have found people experiencing
all those things listed above.

At first glance, the various disciplines with their distinct
vocabularies seem to be referring to radically different
phenomena. Upon closer scrutiny, however, I discovered that
there were some basic principles common to them all which
are, I believe, the major ingredients in the emerging image of
the human being. They are: (1) taking responsibility for our
ableness, (2) the principle of synergy, (3) the power of belief,
(4) the value of altered states of consciousness, and (5) the
power of imagery in an altered state of consciousness.

CHAPTER 5

Owning Our Power

Is William James, along with the many psychologists who have echoed his sentiments, right in saying we are living on only a small percentage of our abilities? I suspect that most of us, even though we are not psychologists, know that to be true. If so, it is not a matter to be taken lightly. No one in business will be successful using only 10 percent of his resources. Can we Chrisians be satisfied with burying 90 percent of the "talents" God has given us? There are ample biblical illustrations of the spiritual consequences of doing that!

To use the metaphor of my dream, the Architect is revealing extra rooms in our houses—ways of utilizing space that perhaps we had not even known was there. Now we are called to move into that space—to take ownership of the power God has created within each of us. If we go back to the original meaning of the word *power,* it means "to be able." Therefore, we need to own our ableness. It is not enough for God simply to reveal our ableness. Just as God freely gives love, it becomes a power in our lives only when we accept that love. God has and is offering unconditional love, but we must appropriate it—own it—for it to become a power in our lives. So it is with our ableness. God is revealing to us vast sources of power that are in and flowing through us, but now it is up to us to appropriate that power, *to accept it, to own it.*

There appear to be two major reasons for our failure to own our power: (1) The status quo is comfortable, and taking greater responsibility is uncomfortable. (2) To claim this kind of ownership of power smacks of a humanistic denial of God's initiative. Let me elaborate on these underlying causes of our inaction.

We are familiar with and comfortable about the notion that we can control the musculature of our bodies to walk and pick up things and to play sports, but it sounds a bit scary to hear that we can also control our blood flow, our heart rate, our blood pressure, et cetera. We have become accustomed to letting the doctor tell us what is wrong with our bodies and what must be done to get our bodies right—whether taking drugs or submitting to surgery. It is frightening to hear that we can play a much more active role in our state of health or disease. It may be easier to continue to believe that I get sick because my boss is too harsh, my job has too much pressure, my spouse doesn't understand, or I was invaded by a "bug," rather than realizing that within my ableness is the capacity to *choose my response* to stress and that this choice, more than stress or "bugs" may be what determines my state of health or illness.

Our capacity to *respond* to life's circumstances—our response-ability—is crucial. I once heard a story about a pastor calling on one of his parishioners who had just been crippled by a serious accident. Expecting the person to be deeply depressed, the pastor sympathetically consoled, "An unfortunate accident like that really colors life." "Yes," replied the parishioner, "but I intend to choose the color!"

We all know similar illustrations of people responding to bad luck with a spirit that inspires us all. Many a story could be told of how differently two people responded to the same kind of misfortune—one grumbling about the bad luck, the other turning the stumbling block into a stepping stone. Someone once said, "If you've been given a lemon, make lemonade."

One of my favorite stories about two different responses to the same situation is that of twin boys who found themselves in an old barn dirty and smelly with manure. One did nothing but complain about the smell of the manure; the other with a twinkle in his eye said, "Hey, there must be a pony loose in here. Let's find him."

Dr. O. Carl Simonton, a radiation oncologist and his wife, Stephanie Matthews-Simonton, a counselor and therapist, are among the most innovative of cancer researchers and therapists. They work at the Cancer Counseling and Research Center in Ft. Worth, Texas, where they have been exploring how stress and psychological factors affect both getting cancer and the course of the disease. Their research indicates the powerful role for our ableness in choosing what our response will be to the onset of disease. Dr. Simonton relates the cases of two of his patients who had almost identical cases of cancer.

They were within a few years of age of each other, and both men had lung cancer that had spread to the brain. One man had had the disease for over a year but had not missed work other than a few hours each time he had a treatment. Early in the development of his disease he had gotten in touch with a lot of things that were causing life to lose meaning for him. He started to spend more time with his family, taking them on business trips with him. I remember him saying one day, "You know I had forgotten that I didn't look at the trees. I hadn't been looking at the trees and the grass and the flowers for a long time and now I do that." It was interesting to watch him. Every week he improved, getting stronger, healthier.

The other man who had lung cancer that had spread to his brain stopped working practically the day he received his diagnosis. He had gone home to sit in front of the television set all day. His wife said that what he did every day was to watch the clock to make sure she gave him his pain medication on time. He was in constant pain. He could not even bring himself to go fishing which was something he liked to do. He died in a short period of time. The other man is still getting healthier day after day. This is the kind of thing we try to show our patients. The treatment for both patients was the same medically, the diagnosis was the same, the patients' ages and physical conditions were almost identical. The difference was in attitude, the way the patients reaced once they knew the diagnosis.[1]

The Simontons point out that it is not just their work that emphasizes the relationship between emotions and cancer. There are over two hundred articles in the medical literature on the same subject. Yet most money for public and private cancer research is spent in looking for external environmental causes of cancer. There is no doubt that external environment plays a role in cancer. But a lot of research indicates that *internal* factors such as attitudes, personality factors, stress management, and beliefs also play a role. The tragedy is that because the majority of funding goes for research of the former, an imbalance of evidence is caused.

George Leonard in his book *The Transformation* tells how the distinguished microbiologist René Dubos "marshalls a great amount of statistical information to show that the presence or absence of germs is only a minor variable in the instance of physical illness. He points out that the microorganisms in our most common diseases are with us always and generally they cause obvious harm only when the conditions of living create some sort of stress."[2]

Dr. Lewis Thomas, president of the Sloan-Kettering Cancer Center in New York and author of *Lives of a Cell,* supports this point of view when he says, "There is a long history of cases that suggest that cancer may be a failure of the immune system and thus hint that a natural mechanism for the elimination of malignancy is lying behind the scenes waiting to be uncovered." The interviewer for the *New York Times Magazine,* responding to Dr. Thomas' statement, said, as if it were a surprise, "You mean that we, ourselves, cause disease and not the bugs?" Dr. Thomas replied simply, "That's right."[3]

Dr. Thomas suggests that, biologically, the external-cause syndrome started with Pasteur, after whom we started to believe that there were "bugs" out there trying to get at us. This idea was reinforced by the Darwinian notion that we are at war with invaders around us and that we can survive only by a major effort to overcome the germs lurking about.

Watching television you would think we lived at bay, in total jeopardy, surrounded on all sides by human-seeking germs, shielded against infection and death only by a chemical technology that enables us to keep killing them off. We are instructed to spray disinfectants everywhere, into the air of our bedrooms and kitchens and with special energy into bathrooms since it is our very own germs that seem the worst kind. We explode clouds of aerosol, mixed for good luck with deodorants, into our noses, mouths, underarms, privileged crannies—even into the intimate insides of our telephones. We apply potent antibiotics to minor scratches and seal them with plastic. Plastic is the new protector. We wrap the already plastic tumblers of hotels in more plastic and seal the toilet seats like state secrets after radiating them with ultraviolet light. We live in a world where the microbes are always trying to get at us to tear us cell from cell and we only stay alive and whole through diligence and fear.

We still think of human disease as the work of an organized, modernized kind of demonology in which the bacteria are the most visible and centrally placed of our adversaries.[4]

The ultimate symbol of this, Dr. Thomas suggests, was how we dealt with the first moon landing. We so bought into the idea that there were hostile germs out there that we went through elaborate isolation procedures with the astronauts as soon as they returned to earth. But Dr. Thomas adds his voice to a growing number of scientists to say, "I have a friendly view of living things. . . . I am of the opinion that all living things are interdependent and that we suffer only for our own mistakes and our overreactions."[5]

One of the most fascinating stories about a person choosing to "own his power" has appeared in both Adam Smith's *Power of Mind* and the *New England Journal of Medicine* (December 23, 1976). It is a story about and told by a patient, not a physician. The patient was Norman Cousins, the well-known and highly respected editor of *Saturday Review.*

Cousins had been on a trip to Russia and began feeling poorly on the flight home. By the time he landed he had a temperature of 104. Within a week he was hospitalized, hardly able to move his neck, arms, or legs. His sedimentation rate was skyrocketing. He was diagnosed as having ankylosing spondylitis of the rheumatoid type, a progressively immobilizing disease. He asked his doctors what his chances were for recovery. The experts conferred and told Cousins that perhaps one patient in five hundred would recover from this disease, although when he pressed them on this matter, none of his doctors could recall having ever seen a patient recover. One of the doctors left a note for another doctor, and when no one was in the room, Cousins read it. "I'm afraid" the note said, "we may be losing Norman."

Cousins began to reflect on his experience in Russia. He had been very tired and under a great amount of stress. He recalled being bothered by diesel fumes of trucks outside his hotel window, as well as the diesel fumes at the airport. Cousins concluded that he had been hit hard by the pollutants, whereas his wife had not (although they were exposed to the same environment) because he had a case of adrenal exhaustion, lowering his resistance. (This is a patient talking, mind you, not a physician.) He had read sometime earlier that the full functioning of the endocrine system, and particularly the adrenal glands, was essential for combating any illness. He also remembered Hans Selye's book *The Stress of Life.* Selye had shown that adrenal exhaustion could be caused by emotional tension such as frustration or suppressed rage. Selye had detailed the negative effects of negative emotions on body chemistry. Cousins struggled with the question, If negative emotions can produce negative chemical changes in the body, *could positive emotions produce positive chemical changes?* Is it possible that love, hope, faith, laughter, confidence, and the will to live have therapeutic value?

A plan began to form in Cousins' mind. He would take the matter into his own hands and try to bring about physical changes by changing his emotions. He decided on two preliminary and necessary steps—very startling proposals—that he would discuss with his doctor. (1) He would have to go off all the toxic medicines being administered to him, which included his pain-killing drugs. If his body was to make a recovery, it could not be held back by the toxic drugs. (2) He also told his doctor that he must be moved out of the hospital to a place more conducive to a positive outlook on life.

So Cousins moved out of the hospital into a hotel room, went off all the drugs, and proceeded to administer some "emotional medicine." He had a movie projector set up in his room and had movies of the Marx Brothers and TV tapes of "Candid Camera" brought in. He began watching the movies and laughing. He found that ten minutes of laughter gave him an hour of pain-free sleep. Cousins also reasoned that vitamin C would help. Reluctantly his doctor administered vitamin C intravenously. Over several months, Cousins recovered and is now totally symptom-free. Norman Cousins concludes his story:

> What we are talking about essentially, I suppose, is the chemistry of the will to live. . . . In Bucharest in 1972, I visited the clinics of Ana Aslan, described to me as one of Rumania's leading endocrinologists. She spoke of her belief that there is a direct connection between a robust will to live and the chemical balances in the brain. . . .
>
> I have learned never to underestimate the capacity of the human mind and body to regenerate even when the prospects seem most wretched. The life force may be the least understood force on earth. . . .
>
> William James said that human beings tend to live too far within self-imposed limits. It is possible that those limits will recede when we respect more fully the natural drive of the human mind and body toward perfectability and regeneration. Protecting and cherishing that natural drive may well represent the finest exercise of human freedom.[6]

The example of Norman Cousins, the research of the Simontons in cancer, the insights emerging from biofeedback, hypnosis, meditation, and the holistic healing modalities, all point toward what is possible when we begin to own our power—our ableness.

Spirit of Synergy: God's Power and You

There is a lot of company for those of us who would rather have the comfort of the old images and the cop-out mentality rather than the scary responsibility of owning our power. There is also, however, fellowship for those who are willing to leave the past behind and follow the God who calls us forth to the Exodus mentality. I suspect there were those who responded to Moses' leadership in leaving Egypt in just these divergent ways. Some no doubt preferred the familiarity of slavery to the unknown risks of the Exodus. Some no doubt went along reluctantly, certain it would lead to disaster. And there were no doubt others who decided to "choose the color" and to keep alive the vision of a land flowing with milk and honey.

The second major reason some of us hesitate to own our power is our assumption that this flies in the face of a humble allegiance to God's power. "Ownership of power" implies we are being saved by our own power rather than by the redemptive power of Jesus Christ. It smacks of a humanistic denial of God's initiative.

What my Architect dream symbolized to me was that God acts as initiator and creator but also calls on me to be a better *steward* of the divinely created reality. The difficulty arises when, because of the limits of our understanding and our vocabulary, we refer to words like *my* or *mine, God* and *Christ,* as though those were mutually exclusive categories. If we believe that God is the creative and sustaining force in all creation, then *no* categories exclude God. Consequently, to talk of *my* power as though it is power separate from God is about as ridiculous as talking of *my* land, as though I could "own" the portion of the earth that my house sits on. Ownership as I am using it here refers to taking responsibility—not as an exclusive claim of sovereignty but as stewardship where all reality is dependent upon God.

The cop-out mentality from a theological point of view would have us thinking that we are being most obedient to God when we think lowly of that which God has created, namely, the human being. I don't think that pays God any compliments! Harvey Cox, the Harvard theologian, has reflected on this subject in his book *On Not Leaving It to the Snake*. Cox suggests that the major sin of humankind is not pride; it is not trying to become more than we were created for but sloth, the unwillingness to face up to all that we are capable of. Cox suggests that the greatest sin is shirking responsibility for full actualization of human potential.

The Christian has been seen as one who humbly doesn't expect too much from himself and who looks externally to God, Christ, the Bible, and the church to bail him out. To be faithful has meant to accept ourselves basically as weak, ineffective, and powerless creatures. But Cox gives us a glimmer of an alternate perspective and bases it in scripture when he says, "The Gospel is first of all a call to leave the past behind and open ourselves to the promise of the future. . . . I believe a careful examination of the Biblical sources will indicate that man's most debilitating proclivity is *not* his pride; it is not his attempt to be more than man, rather it is his sloth, his unwillingness to be everything man was intended to be."[7]

This is not to discount God's initiative in the revelation of Christ in the Bible or in our own lives. It is to suggest that God has not created us as merely passive receptacles. God has created us with a freedom and a will to choose our response to revelation and to our inner reaction to our environment.

I want to mention here what I believe will be one of the major benefits to owning our power, namely, the tranformation of our relationship to experts. We have experts dealing with every aspect of body, mind, and spirit. You name it, and there is surely an expert who can treat it. In the old image of the human being we tended to give unquestioned and absolute authority to these experts for diagnosing and treating any of our ills. This relationship will change as we become more aware of our ableness and begin to own that power. Then, we will have knowledgeable consultants whose advice we seek in order to hear all the messages in our illness. And they may be aware of treatment modalities beyond our experience or knowledge. But we will own the decision since responsibility for our body/mind/spirit is ours. The professional experts will still play valuable roles for us all but as consultants not final authorities.

Ivan Illich has harsh words for what he calls the "imperial professions," that is, professions that encourage dependency and for all practical purposes claim monopolies over certain dimensions of our lives. Let us hope that those of us who consider ourselves professionals will be enablers of personal ableness rather than encourage dependency on us.

CHAPTER 6

The Power
of Synergy

The emerging new image of the human being is in large part
a result of a movement under way to shift from preoccupation
with the separation of reality into parts to an increased
awareness of the essential unity of all reality. I believe we will
move even beyond a sense of unity to the realization that
reality is actually synergetic in nature.

For some time now we in the Western world have been on a
specialization binge. We have been approaching reality in a
reductionist manner, assuming we could learn more by
reducing reality to parts and going deeper and deeper into
smaller and smaller parts.

The illusion of specialization, however, is the illusion of a
group of blind men who were trying to describe an elephant.
One blind man, who was examining the ear of the elephant,
said that an elephant is a large, broad, rough, wide thing
like a rug. Another blind man, who was feeling the trunk
of the elephant, said, "Oh no, you are wrong. I have the facts
about what an elephant really is. It is like a straight and
hollow pipe." But a third blind man, who was feeling

the legs of the elephant, said "No, you're both wrong. An elephant is mighty and firm like a pillar."

We have approached knowledge of the human being in a similar fashion. We have innumerable specialists studying minute parts of the human being. Consequently, we know a great deal about the separate physical parts. But there is a tragic illusion in this, a terribly small view of God's creation—the human being.

Specialization has played a valuable role and has contributed to progress. Nevertheless, the time has come to shift the emphasis. It might even be possible that if we fail to move away from our preoccupation with specialization, our very survival is in question. R. Buckminster Fuller, one of the primary prophets of this movement toward synergy, was reflecting recently on the American Association for the Advancement of Science holding a conference in Philadelphia "where the biologists gathered to discuss the reasons for the extinction of species and the anthropologists met in another hotel to discuss the reasons for the extinction of tribes. Both groups concluded that the primary cause was over-specialization!"[1]

There is an increasing awareness of unity permeating many of our so-called separate disciplines. The French paleontologist and Jesuit priest Teilhard de Chardin predicted this a generation ago. "Like the meridians as they approach the poles, science, philosophy, and religion are bound to converge as they draw nearer to the whole."[2] From the literary world, we hear Arthur Koestler, although apologetic for it, admit that his experience teaches him that there is an "interlocking of all events," a "universal pool," and a unity to all things. Joseph Campbell, a man who has made an extensive study of mythology throughout various races and religions says, "The unity of the race of man exists not only in his biology but also in his spiritual history."[3]

Research psychologist Lawrence LeShan found enough evidence of the common ground of both mystics and physicists in their sense of unity of all things that he wrote a book about the subject, *The Medium, the Mystic and the Physicist.* Albert Einstein, in describing his "unified field theory," said that the deep underlying unity of the universe would be laid bare. The physicist Capra says, "As we study the various models of subatomic physics we shall see that they express again and again, in different ways, the same insight—that the constituents of matter and the basic phenomena involving them are all interconnected, interrelated and interdependent; that they cannot be understood as isolated entities, but only as integrated parts of the whole."[4]

The Italian architect Paolo Soleri writes:

> To cultivate one's soul is then the quest that will back up the skills of the eyes, the ears, the hands and the body with the synergetic power of the mind and ultimately will cast aside the cages of separateness. Separateness is a peculiar invention of man and it is a menace to his position within the evolving universe. . . . Each of us is a universal man or woman because we all are of the universe.[5]

The British scientist James Lovelock who was the first to tell us that the freon released from some of our aerosol cans is endangering the ozone layer of the atmosphere, says that living matter, the air, the oceans, the land, are all parts of a gigantic system which "exhibits the behavior of a single organism, even a living creature."

In a very real sense, the movement toward unity is a rediscovery of a very old insight. Christianity, for instance, has this basic principle as a major biblical theme. "A human body, though it is made up of many parts, is a single unit because all of these parts, though many, make one body" (I Cor. 12:12 JB). "The parts are many but the body is one" (I Cor. 12:20 JB).

The Old Testament word for soul or spirit was *nephesh,* "breath." Like the New Testament word *psyche, nephesh* was meant to convey the whole mental/physical/spiritual personality. Hebraic-Christian thought conceived of the person as a unity rather than a duality. Indeed, Paul pointedly uses the term *soma* for body. *Soma* is the Greek word meaning a psychophysical unity. Theologian D. R. G. Owen summarizes:

> There is little trace of body-soul dualism [in the Bible]; instead, man is regarded as a unity. This personal unity that is man can be called, as a whole, either *soma* (body) or *psyche* (soul) or *sarx* (flesh) or *pneuma* (spirit), . . . but the point is that none of these terms refer to a part of man; they all refer to the whole.[6]

We are not, then, speaking of anything really new when we speak of the human being as a unity. We are only turning to a biblical rather than a Greek philosophical viewpoint.

For the Christian, the symbol of this unity is Jesus Christ, the light of the world who will "unite all things in him, things in heaven and things on earth" (Eph. 1:10). Jesus, among other things, was a mystic. The consciousness of a mystic is one that emphasizes the unity in all things. Jesus emphasized his unity with God when he said, "I and the Father are one." He stressed his unity with all people in the very familiar twenty-fifth chapter of Matthew by instructing his disciples that when they served or did not serve any person in need, it was, in fact, Christ they were serving or not serving, for he is present in the needs of our brothers and sisters.

As I have already stated, it is my conviction that God is moving us beyond a rediscovery of unity to a discovery of *synergy.* Because of our preoccupation with specialization and compartmentalism we are not very familiar with the word or the concept *synergy.* The principle of synergy is that *reality is more than the sum of its parts.*

The Negro spiritual about the ankle bone connected to the leg bone and the leg bone connected to the knee bone provides an apt metaphor. That song starts out a bit beyond specialization by at least identifying the fact that one part is connected to the other. However, the principle of synergy is not reflected in full in the fact that the leg bone is connected to the knee bone. The song finally expresses the idea of synergy when it says, "These bones gonna dance around."

A separate analysis of each bone would give no indication of the possibility of dance. Even the principle of unity—one bone is connected to another bone—does not give an adequate understanding of the phenomenon of dance. Only when the whole organism—body, mind, and spirit—is taken into consideration can we understand and appreciate the possibility of dance. Dancing, that's synergy!

Theologically, synergy is a part of God's very nature. God is the ground of all being. God is that which links together all of life. God, therefore, is the force and the presence that makes whole systems more than we can possibly understand by looking at the individual parts.

The implication of synergy for the emerging new image of the human being is that *humanness* is more than the sum of its parts. Our old image based on specialized data has led us to a notion of humanness that is too small, and we have lived on only 10 percent of our ability. God is calling us to leave behind that deceptive and small image of humanness and to accept the gift of full humanity.

The "old math" of specialization has led us to believe that if you add up the parts, body plus mind plus spirit plus relationships equals four. It is simple logic. Four parts added up equals *four*. But with that "old math" we do an injustice to God's creative and loving power.

The "new math" of synergy has a different result. When body, mind, spirit, and relationships are added up as an intermixture, the total is at least *forty!* Since we have not yet learned how to be full stewards of our gifts, we do not yet love God with all our heart, strength, soul, and mind. However, we know enough to be sure that it is with the concept of synergy, rather than specialization, that we will begin to understand the fullness of humanity.

CHAPTER 7

The Power
of Belief

As he was returning to the city in the early morning, he felt
hungry. Seeing a fig tree by the road, he went up to it and found
nothing on it but leaves. And he said to it, "May you never bear
fruit again"; and at that instant the fig tree withered. The
disciples were amazed when they saw it. "What happened to the
tree" they said "that it withered there and then?" Jesus
answered, "I tell you solemnly, if you have faith and do not
doubt at all, not only will you do what I have done to the fig tree,
but even if you say to this mountain, 'Get up and throw yourself
into the sea,' it will be done, and *if you have faith, everything
you ask for in prayer you will receive."*
—Matt. 21:18-22 JB, italics added

Ascribing such seemingly unlimited power to faith and
belief is very difficult for those of us who are products of
Western scientific cultures. The possibility of Jesus' performing such miracles is one thing, but you and me—that's
something else! We usually rationalize away such statements
by Jesus: He must have been overstating the issue just to

make a point; or, he must mean it allegorically or symbolically but surely not literally. After all, we are a people skilled in critical, analytical thought; we have well-honed skeptical and evaluative faculties. If someone told us that we could get whatever we ask for in prayer—simply by believing strongly enough and having no doubts—why, we would think he was naïve or gullible.

Blake wrote that those who did not believe in miracles surely made it certain that they never would partake of one. Could it be that we who worship science and the so-called rational objective analysis are self-limiting because of our lack of faith in the power of belief ? Many of us have had a hard time accepting any validity for so-called faith healing. But as I mentioned earlier, the more I discovered the powerful role that one's belief structure plays in what actually happens within one's body, the more I become convinced of the legitimacy of some faith healing. Now, scientific research is beginning to verify this role of belief in our lives. It may *be* that we will actually reach the new threshold of awareness with catalytic help from science.

The history of the use of placebos should help to substantiate the power of belief. Patients administered placebos, substances with no known medicinal properties, have been known to improve, apparently because they believed the "medicine" they were taking would help them. Dr. Jerome Frank, a psychiatrist at Johns Hopkins Medical School, reports one study of placebos:

> Patients hospitalized with bleeding peptic ulcers showed 70 percent "excellent results lasting over a period of one year" when the doctor gave them an injection of distilled water and assured them that it was a new medicine that would cure them.[1]

The Power of Belief

There are many studies showing the effectiveness of placebos, in other words, the power of our belief in the doctor or the "medication" he is giving us. But perhaps the most startling statement that Dr. Frank made was this:

> Until the last few decades most medications prescribed by physicians were pharmacologically inert. That is, physicians were precribing placebos without knowing it, so that, in a sense, the history of medical treatment until relatively recently is the history of the placebo effect.[2]

Dr. Thomas Chalmers of Mt. Sinai Medical Center in New York was involved in some research testing the use of vitamin C as a cold preventative. He reports that "the group on placebo who thought they were on vitamin C had fewer colds than the group on vitamin C who thought they were on placebo."[3]

Dr. Simonton is convinced that belief structure plays an important role in the treatment of cancer.

> Our research would indicate that . . . his beliefs about his disease, his treatment and himself are very big factors, having a significant role in the course that his body takes during and after treatment. . . . Most patients see it [cancer] as synonymous with death and something from without that there is almost no hope of controlling. . . . *From the extensive psychological experimentation in expectancy, I can't see how any thinking person can help but see the relationship between what a person believes will happen . . . and the eventual outcome.*[4] (Italics added)

The beliefs held by the family regarding the disease of cancer are also vital because those feelings and beliefs are constantly, subtly, and not so subtly, communicated to the patient—affecting his or her belief. As for the doctor: "Most physicians are not aware of the fact that their thoughts about the treatment and the patient's own ability influence the outcome, but they most definitely do."[5]

In Greek mythology, Procrustes, who was called "The Stretcher," was a robber and a villain who had an iron bed into which he would "fit" his victims. If they were too short, Procrustes would stretch their legs until they fit. If they were too long, he would cut off their legs until they fit. We may not be as cruel as Procrustes, but in terms of how our belief structure deals with reality we are a close brother or sister to "The Stretcher." We generally fit reality into our current belief structure and fail to see or hear anything that contradicts it. The power of our belief structure—whether it is limited or broad—clearly is substantial. The Christian might ask if limited belief is preventing full stewardship of the abilities that God has given.

What Dr. Stanley Krippner calls the "Bannister effect" illustrates how the boundaries of belief affect our actions. You may recall that up until about 1954, no athlete had been able to run a mile in under four minutes. Many tried, but no one could break that barrier. Then Roger Bannister managed to do it, falling exhausted across the tape just split seconds under four minutes. The interesting aspect of this event, however, is that in the year following it, *many* runners managed to break the four-minute mile. What made the difference? It is highly unlikely that all those athletes suddenly improved significantly in terms of skill. What appears to be the case is that the *belief barrier was broken.* Now the runners *knew* it could be done.

Belief structure also appears to play an important role in creativity. Studies of creativity indicate that most major creative insights emerge when the critical mind is relaxed. It would seem that our analytical belief structure, which is valuable for so many things and which necessarily precedes creative insight, just as necessarily must be put out of the way for the creative combination to happen. For, indeed, most creative insight is beyond or outside accepted belief structures. Our belief structure leads us to accept certain ideas as axiomatic. But axioms are deadly to creativity and, I submit, to an openness to the Holy Spirit. Axioms define what is possible and what is impossible. Axioms stop further inquiry or searching. In the history of creative ideas in various fields of human endeavor, major insights and discoveries have usually occurred when someone was bold enough to challenge the axioms of the particular day or within a particular field. When asked how he came onto the theory of relativity, Einstein said simply, "I challenged an axiom."

In Lewis Carroll's *Adventures of Alice in Wonderland,* Alice says, "There's no use trying, one simply can't believe impossible things." "I dare say you haven't had much practice," says the Queen. "When I was your age I always did it for half an hour every day. Why sometimes I believed as many as six impossible things before breakfast." Cultivating the ability to open up our belief structure is one of the important steps to full stewardship of our abilities. We tend to have certain images or beliefs about what we are capable of and what we are not capable of. Those beliefs are shackles that keep us from realizing our potential.

An experiment dealing with the power of belief by Gertrude Schmidler, a psychologist, repeatedly produces the same results. Dr. Schmidler takes a group of college students, for example, and asks them whether they believe in ESP (extrasensory perception). Then she gives them some ESP tests. Time after time, those who believe in ESP score significantly above "chance" on these tests. Those who do not believe in ESP do not, as one might suspect, score simply at "chance level" but significantly *below chance.*

Human beings, it is turning out, simply are not objective machines that can be analyzed or actualized separate from their thoughts and feelings. If we are going to get the maximum potential out of ourselves, we must acknowledge that our beliefs play a major role.

The power of our belief structure is pervasive. It conditions our reality. We discover that the world is not one truth which we have grasped, but as Carlos Castaneda has said:

> Our normal expectations about reality are created by a social consensus. We are taught how to see and understand the world. . . . What we call reality is only one way of seeing the world . . . a way that is supported by a social consensus. [6]

There is little doubt that Hamlet was right when he said, "There are more things in heaven and earth, Horatio, than are dreamt of in your philosophy." For many of us, however, this is a *description,* not a *prescription.* We have defined the situation, so now how do we change belief structure? For instance, if I believe that cancer is a terminal illness, how do I change that belief?

Charlie Brown in a Peanuts cartoon identified the agony many of us share: "How do you do new math," he pleads, "with an old math mind?" That question is certainly much too complex to deal with it completely here. Nevertheless, the Christian gospel has an answer for the Charlie Brown in all of us—the old math mind that is trying to do the new math. It's called repentance.

Unfortunately, the term *repentance* has received a bad press. Generally, we have thought of it in terms of an ultraconservative preacher shouting at us from the radio or television; repentance has usually meant being sorry for something one has done, which has an essentially negative connotation. The Greek word that is translated as "repentance," however, is *metanoia*. What the word really means is a change of mind, or change of consciousness. It seems quite reasonable, then, to relate repentance to a change in belief structure. So, "Repent, brothers and sisters"; God is revealing something new.

The matter of belief structure, however, is a tricky one. Obviously God gave us the capacity for cool, analytical thinking for good reason. There is much of life that is benefitted by these abilities. Yet anyone with an open mind cannot help being impressed with the evidence that indicates that our narrow belief structures have limited life in many ways. There are vast new worlds surrounding the power of belief to be explored. The task of keeping one's analytical faculties well honed while being open to the creative revelations of the Holy Spirit is indeed challenging. If on the one hand, we throw out our critical analytical faculties, we will be gullible and victimized by fraud, fad, and fakery. However, to be too rigid within our current belief structure is arrogant and closes the door on creativity and the work of the Holy Spirit.

For those of us who want to be on an active, searching pilgrimage, in process with a living God, or as Micah put it, "walk humbly with your God" (6:8), there are some marvelous aids emerging in our culture now. There is increasing scientific verification for the expansion of belief structure. There is also an increasing awareness of the possibility of such expansion in the West, and techniques for tapping the intuitive channels for knowing (e.g., meditation and dreams) are available. Consequently, for those who want to participate in a synergetic search for knowledge, utilizing both rational and intuitive forms of perception, there are exciting opportunities.

CHAPTER 8

The Power
of Imagery

Earlier I have stressed that the definition of power is *ableness.* We have explored how our ableness is greatly determined by our belief structure and how it is expanded by the synergetic principle. There is another building block to be used in enlarging our image of the human being: the use of imagery in an altered state of consciousness. Let's first look at each aspect of this technique separately, that is, (1) imagery, and (2) an altered state of consciousness.

First of all, imagery. Editor and publisher Don Gerrard has written:

> If there are two important "new" concepts in 20th Century American Life, they are meditation and visualization. Meditation clears and concentrates the mind; visualization puts an image in it which can profoundly affect the life.[1]

The power of imagery, however, has been recognized and used for a long time. Mike Samuels and Nancy Samuels in their excellent and well-documented book dealing with the history, techniques, and uses of visualization, *Seeing with the Mind's Eye,* told about the use of imagery by American Indian tribes, Canadian Eskimo, the ancient Babylonians, Egyptians, Greeks, and Indian and Oriental civilizations.

> The philosophies of these groups had in common a belief in a spiritual center which formed the universe. This center could be reached by an individual through meditative techniques and visualization. . . . They believed that visualizations manifest themselves as health or disease in the physical body.[2]

Paracelsus, a Swiss physician in the early 1500s, is considered to be the father of scientific medicine and modern drug therapy. Paracelsus believed that the body, mind, and spirit worked together and that imagery was what provided the power of that linkage. "The power of the imagination is a great factor in medicine. It may produce disease in man and in animals, and it may cure them."[3]

Modern medical and scientific research into the linkage of mind, body, and spirit is actually *re*discovering this very old principle. Early in Dr. Simonton's cancer research he reasoned that something might be learned if a study was made of the people who had so-called spontaneous remissions. There are people who suddenly are free of their cancer, for no known medical reason. Medical science cannot explain it. Doctors, understandably, move on to the suffering and ill patients. Consequently, we have learned very little from these unexplained "miracles." Dr. Simonton, however, took a closer look at this phenomenon.

> When we look at spontaneous remission or at unexpectedly good responses and try to figure out what happens in common, we find the same spontaneous occurrence of visualizing oneself being well. You analyze these people. . . . I have not found any

patient that did not go through a similar visualizing process. It might be a spiritual process, God healing them, up and down the whole spectrum. But the important thing was what they pictured and the way they saw things. They were positive, regardless of the source, and their picture was very positive.[4]

Simonton then integrated these insights into the treatment of cancer patients. The patient is told to "see" his cancer in his mind's eye, then to

> visualize the army of white blood cells coming in, swarming over the cancer, and carrying off the malignant cells which have been weakened or killed by the barrage of high energy particles of radiation therapy. . . . These white cells then break down the malignant cells which are then flushed out of the body. Finally, just before the end of the meditation the patient visualizes himself well.[5]

Cancer is not the only problem which seems to be helped with imagery. In the 1930s a German and psychiatrist and neurologist, Dr. J. H. Schultz, developed a technique of using images for physical healing. Called "autogenic therapy," it has been the subject of a good deal of research which demonstrates its effectiveness in treating a variety of chronic diseases. Clinical and experimental hypnosis as well as biofeedback research are filled with similar testimony to the power of imagery. An Italian physician, A. T. W. Simeons, considered one of the leading experts in weight control, uses imagery as part of his treatment, as do many psychologists in the elimination of smoking.

Imagery plays a powerful role in psychological and spiritual reality as well. Freud said, "Thinking in pictures . . . approximates more closely the unconscious processes than does thinking in words."[6] Ignatius, the Bishop of Antioch, and one of the early church fathers, emphasized imagery in his "spiritual exercises." And Vanderbilt Divinity School theologian and dean Sallie TeSelle writes that "Christian language must always be ordinary, contemporary, and imagistic (as it is in the parables)."[7]

Part of of our difficulty in grasping the full power of thinking in images comes from our now outdated and inaccurate notion that fact and fantasy are opposites in terms of reality. We have tended to believe that what we do externally is "reality" and what we simply imagine is somehow "unreal." However, as we learn more about the nature of human reality, we discover that the imagination is a powerful reality, indeed.

The physiologist Edmund Jacobson, in his book *Progressive Relaxation,* reports that his studies showed that when a person simply imagined running, the muscles associated with running actually contracted. Likewise, if we imagine a beautiful relaxing scene, our body actually relaxes. The images we hold in our minds are significantly creating our external and internal reality. Many popular self-help books recognize this principle, however oversimplified they may make it. Athletes know it to be true, as testified to by golf professional Jim Colbert.

> Most people use "mental pictures" to some extent in their daily lives. Few realize the importance of this skill, and even fewer try to develop it. This is a pity, because the best performance is invariably preceded by a "visual picture" of the desired action. Systematically visualizing each shot beforehand helps you establish the desired pattern.[8]

Creative people also testify to the value of imagery. Many creative ideas come in the form of images, as Dr. Jean Houston of the Foundation of Mind Research reminds us.

According to his own statement, Einstein accomplished his most important thought with visual and kinesthetic images, not with words or numbers. Other highly creative people have made similar statements, and much evidence indicates that thinking in images may produce solutions and express ideas that purely verbal thinking cannot.[9]

At the Menninger Foundation in Topeka, Kansas, researchers serendipitously discovered that imagery in an altered state of consciousness could abort migraine headaches. Patients use mental images of "warmth on their hands" to change the blood flow. Biofeedback machines verify that ordinary people can control blood flow and increase their hand temperature, for instance, by ten to fifteen degrees. Since migraine headaches, like Raynaud's disease, are blood flow problems, this kind of imagery power can be significantly useful.

Three generations of Keck men provide an apt illustration of the past, present, and future in terms of getting in touch with the power of imagery as it relates specifically to migraine headaches. My father had a lifetime of periodic suffering and incapacitation from migraines with medical science being of little help. I followed in his footsteps as another "migraine personality" until recently, when I combined meditative prayer with the biofeedback research mentioned above and discovered that I could abort the headaches. Then along comes my son, Jim, who seems to have similar perfectionistic and goal-oriented tendencies. As Jim entered adolescence he began having periodic migraines.

His first migraine came when he was in the sixth grade. I received a call from the school nurse one day informing me that Jim was feeling quite ill. I went to the school to pick him up and on the way home Jim described what happened. It was a classical migraine process: He first had lost a portion of his vision field followed by pain and nausea. Obviously, with Jim in great discomfort, this was not the time to thrust upon him a lot of scientific research data or a meditative prayer workshop. Nevertheless, Jim, being an intellectually curious young man, on his own initiative had sat around the edges of some of our workshops and had asked many questions about the power of imagery. Consequently, I reminded Jim of the fact that his headache was being caused by too much blood pounding in the head through dilated vessels and that by using his imagination, he could change the blood flow, thus relieving him of the pain and discomfort.

When we got home, Jim lay down and I suggested that he try to relax and imagine how it would feel (kinesthetic imagery) to put his hands in a sink of hot water. (Incidentally, the imagination is more powerful than *literally* putting one's hands in hot water.) Ten minutes later Jim came bouncing out of his room totally free of the pain. He had begun to experience the kind of power that all of us have, but few of us have manifested. At one moment he was a young man ahead of his time. In the next moment he was his twelve-year-old self, asking if this was contagious!

The progress within these three generations of migraine headache sufferers is symbolic of the movement toward owning our power and recognizing the power of imagery. What is most important to remember is this is a power within and available to us all. One need not be a Ph.D., a research scientist, or a "blue chip" inner athlete to use it. A housewife in Topeka, a child in Columbus, and you—all have this power.

CHAPTER 9

The Power
of Altered States
# of Consciousness

The subject matter of this chapter is extremely important if we are really going to understand, let alone tap, the vast amount of our abilities that lie dormant. We exist in a culture that has given us little help in understanding altered states of consciousness. Quite the contrary, in fact. Our Western culture has promulgated a bias for ordinary waking consciousness and against altered states of consciousness.

Perhaps the understanding of what is to follow would be aided if we took a brief imaginative trip together to see Mr. Wes Culture.

The Power of Altered States of Consciousness

Once upon a time we went to visit a relative, Wes Culture. When we arrived, we were startled to notice that he was sitting on the front porch with all his furniture.

"Wes, why are you and your telephone, your kitchen table, your living room furniture, all out here on the porch?" I asked.

"I live out here," Wes replied, "at least during the daytime. I only go into the house at night to sleep." Wes was frantically searching through a stack of books that were at one end of the porch. He seemed quite irritated and tense, obviously very intent upon finding something. But he was failing to find what he was looking for.

"Can I help?" I inquired. "What is it you are looking for?"

"The Books of Meaning and Purpose," Wes snapped. "It is a series, and I have found some of them, but some are missing. I think the missing books are inside the house where I sleep."

I felt a little silly asking, but it was the only logical question: "Then, why, Wes, are you looking for them out here on the porch?"

"Because," Wes replied, "there is more light out here!"[1]

A cursory look at how we approach the search for meaning and purpose reveals just how close a relative Wes Culture really is. We have looked almost exclusively out in the waking consciousness and relegated the inside of the house to the unconscious state of sleep and paid very little attention to that!

Robert Ornstein, in *The Psychology of Consciousness,* elaborates on this observation. He suggests that if we were awake only during the daytime we would know nothing about the stars. In fact, if someone who had been awake during the night came to tell us about the stars and to tell us that there was a scientific exploration of the heavens called astronomy, it would sound incredible. We would perhaps doubt his sanity and surely ascribe such talk to the occult.

That is precisely what we in Western culture have done regarding altered states of consciousness. We have by and large been unfamiliar with them, feared them, refused to consider them "scientific," and assigned labels to them like "occult" that allow us to dismiss them. Yet it is increasingly clear that altered states of consciousness are the key to releasing vast portions of our untapped abilities and are certainly involved in a full life of meaning and purpose.

Charles Panati, a science writer for *Newsweek* who has been a radiation physicist at Columbia University and head physicist at RCA, writes: "We are more than the mere composite of our wakeful perceptions for the purely 'wakeful person' is only half human. Perhaps as research into the paranormal accelerates, the day will come when the prefix 'para' will be dropped altogether. After all, it is only an admission of our present inability to grasp the full spectrum of things that are humanly possible."[2] If this sounds very confusing to you, don't feel bad. You are simply the logical product of the mainstream of our culture.

Contemporary Christianity, education, and medical care, for instance, almost totally ignore the potential in altered states of consciousness. They have consequently been missing vast areas of rich resources by which a person can find meaning spiritually, gain and use knowledge, and play an active role in creating and maintaining health. There is clear evidence now that the new image of the human being beginning to appear over the horizon includes the exploration and use of altered states of consciousness. Any area of society that purports to be helpful to human development will either be responsive to this or it will become obsolete.

Like any movement of substance, this movement has roots

in our past and in our present. Let's take a look at some of these roots, past and present evidence of the importance of altered states of consciousness for the full and abundant life.

CHRISTIANITY

Christianity's most important roots are personal and corporate experiences—many including altered states of consciousness—rather than its institutionalized liturgy and theologies. There is a restlessness evident—particularly among the youth—for getting back to the experiential. Anyone who reads the Bible can see why William James said, "Personal religious experience has its roots and centre in mystical states of consciousness."[3]

Moses, receiving the Ten Commandments, was clearly having a mystical experience. And throughout the Bible, dreams are regarded as a primary way in which people experienced God in their lives. In little more than a chapter of the Gospel of Matthew (1:18–2:23), dreams bear significantly on the course of Jesus' life four times, and a fifth dream revelation affects the men who brought the baby Jesus gifts.

First of all, Joseph was going to leave Mary when he found that she was pregnant before they were married. "An angel of the Lord appeared to him in a dream," however, and changed his mind by revealing the significance of her pregnancy. After Jesus' birth, a second appearance of an angel in a dream warned Joseph to take Mary and Jesus to Egypt because Herod was going to seek the life of Jesus. Next, Joseph was notified of Herod's own death through a dream and was told it would now be safe to return to Israel. Just before they arrived, Joseph was warned again through a dream and re-routed his journey to the region of Galilee, to Nazareth, so that Jesus' return to Israel would follow the scriptures.

Jesus himself was obviously familiar with an altered state of consciousness in a number of mystical experiences. Paul's Damascus Road experience also probably took place in an altered state of consciousness. My Methodist heritage won't allow me to ignore John Wesley's experience at Aldersgate when he felt his heart "strangely warmed"—an altered state of consciousness that launched a religious revival in England. I suspect that one could trace every major religious revival to the energy that comes from a deeply personal experience of an altered state of consciousness.

HEALING

Many ancient cultures used altered states of consciousness in bringing about the changes that would facilitate healing. And today, even though our medical practitioners do not use or generally accept as efficacious any altered state of consciousness, I have had several people tell me that such an experience accompanied a dramatic healing. We generally pass off such occurrence with the label "spontaneous remission."

Some of the more unorthodox healers of our culture—faith healers and psychic healers—tell of and have electroencephalographic verification of being in an altered state of consciousness at the time of the healing.

Arigó, the Brazilian peasant who had such extraordinary healing and diagnostic abilities, could not even remember some of the early incidents of healing when he performed surgery because he was in a trance. Later, however, he was able to be more aware of his actions, though he was still in some sort of altered state of consciousness as he was being told what to do by "Dr. Fritz" who spoke into his ear. Edgar Cayce, too, performed his extraordinary diagnostic work while in a trance state.

In addition to these examples, the Menninger Foundation

experiments with an Indian yogi, Swami Rama, and with Jack Schwarz, a native of the Netherlands, indicate both were *able* to perform extraordinary tasks requiring regulation of physical and mental states. And both were shown to be using an altered state of consciousness to accomplish these tasks.

HYPNOSIS

I referred earlier to my research in clinical and experimental hypnosis, which uses, of course, an altered state of consciousness. Let me relate another personal experience. Shortly after returning from some intensive training in hypnosis, my daughter Krista was hit on the eyebrow with a baseball in a playground accident. It was quite a blow, and her forehead swelled considerably. She was about ten years old when this happened, and the accident made her hysterical. Between her hysteria and the pain, she would not let us put ice on her forehead to keep down the swelling.

I was surprised, in spite of what my training had taught me, to find how quickly Krista followed my instructions, entered a relaxed state of mind, stopped crying, and fully conscious, let us apply an ice pack. The trauma was over as quickly as it had started, and we were able to control the swelling. Here, then, is another illustration of the value of an altered state of consciousness brought about through relaxation.

CREATIVITY

Accounts of creative people and how they come up with their ideas also provide substantial testimony to the value of an altered state of consciousness. What seems to happen in the creative process is, first of all, the hard work on a problem or challenge. Second, the material gathered through this work seeps down into the unconscious where the axioms and rigid belief structures exert less constricting influence. Then, after a period of incubation, the creative idea emerges. The circumstances under which the creative idea actually comes forth are significant. Usually, the person is in a situation away from the problem or challenge, and frequently he or she is in an altered state of consciousness, such as meditation or a dreaming state.

Perhaps the major discovery in organic chemistry, the benzene ring, came to Kekulé while he was dozing in front of the fireplace. Nobel prizes have been won on the basis of material emerging in dreams. Niels Bohr, the physicist, was helped by a dream in conceptualizing the structure of the atom. Dreams also played major roles in the creativity of Mozart, Robert Louis Stephenson (Dr. Jekyll and Mr. Hyde was first a dream—or a nightmare!), Abraham Lincoln, Walt Whitman, Ralph Waldo Emerson, Plato, William Blake, Schubert, to name only a few. The arena of creativity is clearly one more that witnesses to the value of altered states of consciousness.

EXTRASENSORY PERCEPTION

I won't go into a long discussion here about the pros and cons in the debate about so-called ESP. I am convinced, however, that if anyone with an open mind will study the scientific research being applied now to psychic phenomena, there will be little doubt that all of us have many abilities we have thought only a few extraordinary people possessed.

The striking thing about ESP phenomena is that what "exceptional" people experience in their ordinary state of consciousness, the rest of us common folk can (and do) experience in altered states of consciousness. Consequently, a good case can be made for this not being "extra" ability, only that which is available in states of consciousness that we ordinarily do not value or pay attention to. For instance, because most of us in our culture do not enter into the meditative state of consciousness or pay heed to our dreams, we may be unaware that telepathic, clairvoyant, and precognitive thoughts are in and with us almost daily.

The story that follows, if it had happened to a lesser figure than Charles Lindbergh, would, I'm afraid, be simply dismissed by a culture unfamiliar with altered states of consciousness. But in this instance, when a folk hero relates an extraordinary experience, we listen more attentively.

> While I'm staring at the instruments, during an unearthly age of time, both conscious and asleep, the fuselage behind me becomes filled with ghostly presence—vaguely outlined forms, transparent, moving, riding weightless with me in the plane. I feel no surprise at their coming . . . without turning my head, I see them as clearly as though in my normal field of vision. There's no limit to my sight—my skull is one great eye, seeing everywhere at once. . . .
>
> These phantoms speak with human voices . . . familiar voices, conversing and advising on my flight, discussing problems of my navigation, reassuring me, giving me messages of importance unattainable in ordinary life.[4]

ATHLETICS

The realm of athletics is another witnessing to the value of altered states of consciousness. The athletic "psyche-up"—the way an athlete prepares mentally for a contest—is actually the skill of manipulating consciousness so as to induce better concentration, quicker reflexes, greater strength, and more endurance.

All these benefits are possible if we move slightly into a more "hyper" state of consciousness. An emergency does this automatically for us, initiating the "flight or fight" response. We've all heard such stories as that of a slightly built woman lifting a heavy weight off a child who is being crushed. Greater strength is possible in an altered state of consciousness—one at the opposite extreme from a relaxed altered state but nonetheless altered from our ordinary state of consciousness. An athlete simply enters this state intentionally.

One might think that the rough contact sport of football would not lend itself to the exceptional experience of an altered state of consciousness. Nevertheless, John Brodie, former quarterback for the San Francisco Forty-Niners and Most Valuable Player in the National Football League in 1970, tells the kind of story we are not accustomed to reading in the morning paper's sport pages.

Often in the heat and excitement of a game, a player's perception and coordination will improve dramatically. At times, and with increasing frequency now, I experience a kind of clarity that I've never seen adequately described in a football story. Sometimes, for example, time seems to slow way down, in an uncanny way, as if everyone were moving in slow motion. It seems as if I have all the time in the world to watch the receivers run their patterns and yet I know the defensive line is coming at me just as fast as ever. I know perfectly well how hard and fast those guys are coming and yet the whole thing seems like a movie or dance in slow motion. It's beautiful.[5]

BIOFEEDBACK

Biofeedback is another use of an altered state of consciousness that has been discussed at some length already. It is a very effective example because it uses a scientifically accepted means (electronic instrumentation) to verify altered state of consciousness. Consequently, it might be helpful to elucidate this more fully.

The electroencephalograph (EEG) is the particular instrument that is used to "measure" states of consciousness. This machine measures the electrical impulses coming off the surface of the brain. On a paper read-out the electrical impulses are recorded as waves, therefore being called brain waves. The waves, or electrical impulses, are measured in cycles per second. Brain-wave researchers have identified the ordinary state of consciousness (called *beta*) and the other states of consciousness (designated *high beta, alpha, theta,* and *delta*) according to their correlation with the frequency of the cycles per second. Charting the different states of consciousness according to brain-wave frequencies may help visualize these correlations:

State of Consciousness	EEG Cycles Per Second
High Beta	25 and up
Beta	12–25
Alpha	8–12
Theta	4–8
Delta	0–4

I want to stress that this model is not to be accepted too dogmatically. Brain-wave research is in its infancy, and this analysis is not necessarily the last word in interpreting the brain's activities. Using this simple categorization can be a first step toward understanding states of consciousness.

High Beta. This state of consciousness is characterized by a fast brain-wave rate that represents a more "hyper" condition than what we experience during most of a usual day. It would be present, in all likelihood, in an emergency, in an athletic "psyche-up," or in an ecstatic experience. It would not be unusual to find people in high beta relating experiences or displaying physical abilities that seem extraordinary. They are, in fact, literally out of the ordinary state of consciousness and capable of experiences and actions normally considered impossible.

Beta. This is the label brain-wave researchers have given to our normal state of consciousness. It is in beta (13-25 cycles per second of electrical activity coming off the scalp) that most of us spend our waking day. For instance, if you had an EEG hooked up to you right now while you're reading this book, it would probably indicate you are in beta. Beta is characterized essentially by an external orientation, critical and analytical thinking, and normal everyday physical activity.

Alpha. This state is represented by a slower brain-wave pattern, between 8 and 12 cycles per second. An alpha state of consciousness is produced by becoming deeply relaxed, getting rid of muscular and mental tension and, for most people, closing the eyes. It is a turning away from the outside world and a turning into the inside world. This state of consciousness, as recorded by the EEG, is that of many meditators. It is also the precursor of sleep for most people.

Theta. At a frequency of 4 to 7 cycles per second, this is a yet deeper, even more relaxed state of consciousness. It is the deepest state of consciousness that most people are able to achieve in meditation and often includes dreamlike imagery that bubbles into the conscious awareness from that which was previously unconscious.

Delta. Reflected by 0 to 4 cycles per second, delta is the deepest state of consciousness represented by brain-wave patterns and is usually experienced, except for some few "blue chip" meditators, only in deep sleep.

All of us experience the alpha, theta, and delta states of consciousness when we sleep, but for the nonmeditator, that's about the only time they are experienced. One need reflect only briefly to conclude that we have a cultural bias for beta. High beta has drawn praise in the context of an emergency or in athletic competition, but is clearly suspect in religious experience, for it seems to result in such phenomena as visions or speaking in tongues. Of course, there are ample biblical illustrations that sound suspiciously like experiences in a high beta state of consciousness (e.g., Paul's Damascus Road experience), but those are safely enshrined in history!

Alpha, theta, and delta are all right for sleeping, but we have also clearly been a culture that does not value either meditation or dreams. Again, we find much biblical evidence for the importance of these states of consciousness, but there is little evidence the contemporary church believes they are relevant for modern life.

Another chart can identify in which states of consciousness different types of experiences occur:

Ecstatic experiences Emergency reactions Athletic "psyche-up"	HIGH BETA 25 and up	↑ AWAKE ↓
Ordinary waking consciousness Intellectual, verbal activity Verbal prayer	BETA 12–25	
Meditative state of conscious- ness Meditative Prayer Dream state of consciousness	ALPHA 8–12	↑ USUALLY ASLEEP ↓
Many forms of healing Hypnosis ESP experiences	THETA 4–8	
Deep sleep	DELTA 0–4	

Spending all our waking hours in beta and experiencing alpha or theta only when we are asleep is similar to our friend Wes Culture's spending his days out on the porch.

What follows in Part III is the specific and practical innovation that has been developed at New Wineskins Center for Research and Development. It is a concept and practice of Christian prayer utilizing the meditative state of consciousness. There are enormous and meaningful benefits for the person who adds the possibilities inherent in meditative prayer to his or her life.

PART III

TOWARD A LARGER IMAGE OF PRAYER

CHAPTER 10

On Not Sleeping Through a Revolution

Remember Rip Van Winkle, the lazy farmer who lived in the Catskill Mountains above the Hudson River? Rip drank some magic wine and slept for twenty years. When he fell asleep, George III ruled America, and when Rip awoke, his country was a republic. He had slept through a revolution! There is a revolution occurring in our understanding of the human being. Emerging from that revolution is a much larger image than we held previously.

If our educational systems sleep through this revolution, they will continue to approach learning as though beta consciousness is the only legitimate way of gaining or processing knowledge. They will continue, if asleep, to approach "physical education" as though it has to do only with the larger muscles of the body and sports. They will continue to ignore a person's capacity for learning how to orchestrate a harmony between body, mind, and spirit and the marvelous rewards of that effort.

If our health care systems sleep through this revolution,

they will continue to process the human being as if body, mind, and spirit were separate, distinct entities and never fully consider the person's own ability to create and maintain health. They will continue to be disease-oriented rather than health-oriented.

If our political systems sleep through this revolution, they will continue in the self-destructive preoccupation with sovereignty and never discover the synergetic interdependence of the "global village."

Because of my close relationship with the Christian church all my life and my professional role as a United Methodist clergyman, I have a particular interest in making sure the church does not pull a Rip Van Winkle in this matter of the emerging new image of the human being. If we are not to sleep through this revolution we will be developing new ways to enable spiritual growth.

Willis Harman of Stanford University, a leading thinker in the study of cultural institutions, suggests that when institutions or systems no longer serve the purpose they claim to serve, they die. They die not so much by violent overthrow as by the subtle loss of legitimacy. If the church dies, it will certainly not be from an aggressive attack by revolutionaries. Rather its death will be brought about by people's simply withdrawing legitimacy. Many people in our time have already withdrawn legitimacy from the church for anything besides baptizing, marrying, and burying. If the church does not enable spiritual growth and a just and loving society based upon the larger image of humanity that God is currently revealing, then increasing numbers will take away their support, and the church will sink into a fatal malaise.

The commandment for the church's life is very old and very biblical, but it must be carried out in light of God's revelation in our time. Jesus stated the first and greatest commandment:

"You must love the Lord your God with all your heart, with all your soul, with all your mind and with all your strength. The second is this, you must love your neighbor as yourself. There is no commandment greater than these." Here Jesus ties together two of the main themes of the New Testament: love of God and full use of potential for love. We are called to love with *all* our capabilities, yet we know that we have been living on only a small percentage of them.

The revolution that has been taking place—or revelation, if you will—shows us *how* we can begin to use some of that untapped potential. The crisis of legitimacy for the church today has come about not so much because the central message of the gospel is missing but because it is not guiding us in the *means* of making that message a living part of ourselves. Dr. Harman provides a helpful image:

> If one understands the dynamics and develops sufficient skill, he can learn to ride a surfboard. However, if there is no wave, he cannot create one; if there is a wave, he cannot stop it. But if there is a wave and if he can ride a surfboard, then he is in a position very different from the one he would be in without that skill.[1]

God is making waves—waves that can carry us to greater attempts at loving with *all* our being. We need new skills at riding the waves—skills of utilizing altered states of consciousness in synergetic cooperation with our ordinary state of consciousness.

There is a biblical image that points in the same direction: "Nor do people put new wine into old wineskins; if they do, the skins burst, the wine runs out, and the skins are lost. No; they put new wine into fresh skins and both are preserved" (Matt. 9:17 JB).

God is constantly fermenting new wine of the spirit, a new wine which can satisfy our thirst for wholeness (at-one-ment) in ourselves, with our brothers and sisters in humankind, and with the God who is the ground and source of all life. But as the gospel writer put it, we need new wineskins for the new wine. In other words, the church, if it is to retain legitimacy as a spiritual enabler, must be creating new wineskins to aid its people in tasting the new wine of the spirit. Christian prayer is desperately in need of new wineskins—new methodologies that incorporate God's newest revelations, new ways to enable us to love with *all* our heart, strength, soul, and mind.

In the very spirit of synergy, this is not in any way to demean the older methodologies. There is nothing wrong with the verbal prayers we have utilized for so long in the beta state of consciousness. We know now, though, that if that's *all* we're doing, it's not enough! Prayer, if it is to be responsive to the larger image of the human being, must be holistic, utilizing many states of consciousness in a synergetic, full actualization of body/mind/spirit.

The Latin root for the word *religious* means "to bind together," Yet in prayer, what may be the most religious of all activities, we have separated out a certain type of consciousness for exclusive use, ignoring the other types of consciousness.

It might be helpful to attempt a definition of prayer. And since prayer is communion with God, one cannot avoid at least an implicit definition of God. The concept of God that I am assuming here is one that is more inclusive than exclusive. It does not engage in the argument as to whether God is immanent or transcendent, for God is both. The tendency to argue for a "location" of God, either "out there" (a transcendent God), or "in here" (an immanent God) is too limiting and is counterproductive. This either/or mentality inevitably leads to a debate over whether one is a theist on the one hand or a humanist on the other. Our propensity for dichotomy has led us to draw a distinction between an external God and an internal God, heaven and earth, spirit and matter. For the most part, these distinctions have been divisive, misleading in their oversimplification, and of more harm than good.

Immanence literally means "living or operating within." Certainly God is within, but God is not *limited* to the within. *Transcendence* literally means "existing apart from the material universe." Certainly God is more than matter, but in God matter is spiritualized and God is in matter.

Christianity has an apt symbol for this unity of God and human, matter and spirit, immanence and transcendence; it's called the Incarnation, literally, "God in flesh." As in so many cases, the answer for our need in modern times has roots in biblical and ancient symbols. Jesus was the Christ precisely because he was the revelation of the union of matter and spirit, God in flesh, man attuned to the spirit of love. We got off on the wrong track, however, in thinking all that applied only to Jesus. We then elevated Jesus out of the realm of the human and reestablished the dichotomy.

Norman Pittenger was on the right track when he said that we should reevaluate our idea of the Incarnation as part of our doctrine of man. The Incarnation should illuminate human nature, Pittenger tells us, as well as describe Jesus Christ. God is incarnate in each one of us and therefore "in him we live and move and have our being."

Suffice it to say here that God is viewed as very personal *and* very cosmic. He is in us and with us and beyond us. The psalmist expresses it in elegant fashion:

> Where can I escape from thy spirit?
> Where can I flee from thy presence?

If I climb up to heaven, thou art there;
if I make my bed in Sheol, again I find thee.
If I take my flight to the frontiers of the morning
    or dwell at the limit of the western sea,
even there thy hand will meet me
    and thy right hand will hold me fast. (Ps. 139:7-10 NEB)

Prayer, therefore, is not the moment when God and human are in relationship, for that is always. *Prayer is taking initiative to intentionally respond to God's presence.* We can do that with words or with feelings, with intellect or with intuition, alone or with others.

I have no desire to discredit any of the various types of prayer—quite the contrary. I affirm verbal prayer as well as prayer that takes the form of social action. It is clear that one cannot be responsive to the Christian gospel and ignore the oppressed, the hungry, and the infirm. The support of justice and humanness in our world is certainly a form of prayer and essential to communion with God. Rabbi Abraham Heschel has said, "When I marched with Martin Luther King in Selma, I felt my legs were praying."

It is clear that most of us Western Christians have been accustomed to verbal and social action prayers using beta consciousness but that we have little familiarity with the other states of consciousness that can be used for prayer. The emerging larger image of the human being reveals the powerful capacities of the alpha and theta states of consciousness—this is where the church today needs a new wineskin! Although the average Christian often associates meditation (alpha-theta) with Eastern religions, a Christian concept of prayer can be applied to the meditative state of consciousness just as it can to our ordinary state of consciousness. God did not create altered states of consciousness for only the exclusive use of the Hindus and Buddhists to use.

I have spent the past four years reserching and developing a meditative type of Christian prayer so that Christians can drink of this new wine of the spirit and so that the church can enable this to take place. What follows is an attempt to share with you some insights into this kind of prayer, one that I hope you will find enabling of rich and exciting communion with God.

CHAPTER 11

How Meditative
Prayer Was Developed

I would like to take up my personal story again in the summer of 1973. I had gone through the "tour by the Architect," and although I had had the dream predicting all this back in January, I had forgotten about it and had not yet discovered my notes on it (I found the notes about the dream in the fall). I had also experienced the miracle of pain relief and now was on summer vacation.

I was with my family and our friends the Murphys and the Millers in northern Wisconsin, enjoying the sun, the water, and some golf (Cleo would even let me win once in a while). All the thoughts and reflections of the phenomenal year just past were lingering in my mind as I lay on the beach one afternoon. All of a sudden, it hit me like a bolt of lightning—I could not go back to ministry as usual. I just had to explore this experience further and see what implications there would be for a concept and practice of prayer. I was actually dozing on the beach, and it was as if God said, "No Rip Van Winkle act for you, fellow. There's a revolution going on and you have some work to do!"

108

I went back to First Community Church in Columbus, Ohio, determined to act on that impulse. Fortunately, there were beautiful people there who could respond to a vision, and a three-year research project was launched.

My research has been broad and interdisciplinary, based on the belief that God ferments the new wine of the spirit in many places—some with religious labels but also some with scientific, medical, psychological, or parapsychological labels. In fact, I was particularly suspicious of the tunnel vision that can result from too parochial a search. I simply do not believe that God separates life into religious and secular categories and restricts revelation to the former. Such categorizations are more the result of our need than a true picture of God's structure of reality.

God is not an egotist. God has not created us with a tattoo across our back: An Original Creation of God's Made in Heaven. Nor does God have a signature written across a sunset or a full moon reflecting across a body of water. We are not forced to give God credit. Revelations are marketed under various brand names since God knows some of us will listen to science; some to machines; some to psychology; and yet others, to religion.

I tried to take a careful look at many systems throughout the history of human inquiry that tried to define and describe the deep workings of the body/mind/spirit. The goal was to find out what force was at work underneath the particular vocabulary and belief structure of each system. The study encompassed traditional concepts of Christian prayer, Eastern forms of meditation, biofeedback, clinical and experimental hypnosis, psychic research, dream research, Jungian psychology, transpersonal psychology, quantum physics, bioenergetics, split-brain theory, psychosynthesis, and many others. Where were the common, substantive insights of the deep body/mind/spirit that God was revealing in a broad cross-section of seemingly diverse field of inquiry?

The insights coming out of this research were constantly tested against the following criteria:

1. Do they legitimately fit into a Christian concept of prayer?
2. Can they be taught to the average person in our churches?
3. Are they helpful in terms of spiritual growth and development?

The results of the research have led to the development of what I call *meditative prayer,* that is, a form of Christian prayer utilizing the meditative state of consciousness. Meditative prayer has been shaped and honed by the many people in the First Community Church congregation and field-tested through workshops with some five thousand Christians, both lay and clergy, in churches of various denominations and ranging geographically from Massachusetts to Hawaii, from Ontario, Canada, to Florida and Texas. At the same time this was going on, a committee of seminary deans analyzed meditative prayer regarding its implications for theological education, and a group of biblical scholars and theologians, headed by John Cobb, Jr., of Claremont School of Theology, made an in-depth critique of and contribution to meditative prayer.[1]

Meditative prayer is, therefore, intentionally a Christian concept and practice of prayer. It has been created with the hope that it will be a methodology that can enable individuals, and the church as an institution, to taste the new wine that is fermenting today. This statement is meant to indicate *focus* not *exclusivity.* Certainly these methods can be used by non-Christians. I don't believe God makes the new wine *only* for those with a particular theology. Nevertheless, meditative prayer is a new wineskin for use within the Christian church.

Because meditative prayer is a blend of insights emerging from a variety of fields, and because we have been so accustomed to labeling and categorizing experiences without much discrimination between the label and the content, it is easy to misunderstand meditative prayer. Misunderstanding will result, however, only if one looks at parts rather than the whole. In meditative prayer, for instance, it is possible to eliminate the perception of pain. If someone were to lift that part *out of context,* it would be logical to think, Well, that's not prayer; that's self-hypnosis. Likewise, in meditative prayer one can change the blood flow within one's body so as to abort a migraine headache. Looking at this, again *out of context,* one could say, That's not prayer; it's biofeedback. Also in meditative prayer it is possible to experience the kind of communication with others that could lead one to say, That's not prayer; it's telepathy.

Yet taken as a whole, it is a concept of prayer that focuses on communion with God—within which amazing self-actualization and linkage with others is possible. None of the "systems" have a corner on the vocabulary that describes God's creations. Meditative prayer is simply one system available for Christians, one that uses the vocabulary and symbolic framework of this particular faith.

In the development of meditative prayer, it soon became obvious that there are two pitfalls that need to be carefully avoided. One is an overemphasis on the healing capabilities of the body/mind/spirit synergy. Because my experience with back pain was the catalyst for my getting into this work, and because it can come across as a rather remarkable happening, it is natural for people to emphasize this element—particularly if they, too, need healing. Meditative prayer can facilitate the remarkable healing that is possible when body/mind/spirit is orchestrated. However, this is only *one* aspect of a complete concept of prayer.

The other pitfall is to be carried away by the psychic phenomena that are experienced in altered states of consciousness. Again, although these are natural experiences in the larger image of the human being, they are not the only—or the most important—experiences.

To avoid these pitfalls, we need to keep in mind that all meditative prayer is first and foremost *communion with God.* Later I will discuss four types of meditative prayer which are each based on a different need in our relationship with God. A balance among these types of prayer should be maintained in order to keep meditative prayer true to the concept of Christian prayer, and the cornerstone of them all is God's central position.

CHAPTER 12

Techniques
of Meditative Prayer

Because as Western Christians, most of us have not been accustomed to using the meditative state of consciousness, there was a need to define the basic techniques that would help beginning meditators learn and develop their skill. In researching carefully the many systems that use the meditative, or alpha-theta, state of consciousness I was looking for a common process that could be freed from the parochial jargon of the respective systems. I found that whether a system used a "mantra" or "autogenic phrases" or "induction," the basic process being used was one of (1) relaxation, (2) concentration, and (3) imagery.

Let's take a closer look at these three building blocks of meditative prayer so that you can practice and develop these skills. Remember Willis Harman's image of the surfboard and the wave? Relaxation, concentration, and imagery are the skills by which you can ride that wave.

I am aware that to speak of techniques in Christian prayer may be anathema to some people. Nevertheless, I believe such a discussion is necessary for at least two reasons. First of all, whereas verbal prayer involves no techniques that we are not already familiar with, namely, ability to think logically and to phrase our thoughts, meditative prayer involves an altered state of consciousness—which most of us are not familiar with. It is necessary, therefore, to learn techniques that will enable us to enter an altered state of consciousness. Second, just as freedom and creativity in playing the piano are dependent upon hours of skill development, so also is the maximum freedom and creativity in meditative prayer dependent upon a disciplined practice and development of the techniques of relaxation, concentration, and imagery—the techniques through which we alter consciousness and begin to use the synergy of the deep body/mind/spirit.

RELAXATION

The stress and tension that builds up in the body and mind because of everyday emotional concerns and intellectual preoccupation create static in the spiritual airwaves. In order to get into a meditative state of consciousness as well as to be free for the creative possibilities in a meditative prayer, one needs to be able to achieve at least temporary relief from this stress and tension. Relaxation must be both physical and mental—a nonattachment to muscular stress and tension, intellectual preoccupation, and emotional concerns. Because of the mind/body/spirit interrelatedness, it is not only inappropriate but impossible to effectively separate relaxation of the psyche and of the soma.

Too much stress leads eventually to *dis-stress. Dis-ease* for too long a time leads to *disease.* Consequently, there are direct health benefits from regular relaxation, even without engaging the power of concentrated imagery. There is an increasing amount of medical research verifying this connection between stress and disease. In fact, as I survey the data from such research, I am prone to speculate theologically that God did not intend the mind and body to be constantly "in gear," revving the muscular and mental motors. God evidently has created human beings who remain healthier without the extreme stress and tension that has become characteristic of our culture. If you were to put sand in the gas tank of your car, the engine would not remain "healthy" for very long. The creator of the automobile did not intend the engine be run on sand. Likewise, if we can make a theological deduction from the current physiological research regarding effects of stress, it would seem that the Creator of our bodies did not intend them to run on the level of stress typical in our culture.

Another recognition of the relationship of body and mind and the importance of relaxation comes from tennis professional Timothy Gallwey. Although referring to the "inner game of tennis," Gallwey's words are applicable to meditative prayer.

Quieting the mind means less thinking, calculating, judging, worrying, fearing, hoping, trying, regretting, controlling, jittering or distracting. The mind is still when it is totally here and now in perfect oneness with the action and the actor. . . .

At this point the question naturally arises: "How can I still my mind?" . . . The answer is simple: just stop! As an experiment the reader might want to put down this book for a minute and simply stop thinking . . .

The first skill to learn is the art of letting go the human inclination to judge ourselves and our performance as either good or bad.

The quiet mind cannot be achieved by means of intellectual understanding. Only by the *experience* of peace in a moment when the mind is relatively still is one sufficiently encouraged to let go more completely the next time. Very gradually one begins begins to trust the natural process which occurs when the mind is less and less active.[1]

It may be that one of the major reasons some of us have difficulty really letting go of the stress of thinking is that we are short on *trust*—trust in God and in our communion with God when we are not "in charge" or "on guard." Can we relax our intellect, trusting that without holding tenaciously to our beliefs about God, we may encounter God in a new way? It is not easy to stop doing and just be; to stop thinking and just be; to stop judging and just be! It is not easy—and that is precisely why we need to practice it.

Ernest Wood, a man very familiar with Eastern forms of meditation, has written: "It is not healthy to be thinking all the time. Thinking is intended for acquiring knowledge or applying it. It is not essential living."[2] Now that *really* sounds anathema to our Protestant work ethic, our accomplishment-oriented mentality! But we will realize very little divine guidance in our lives if we don't *stop thinking and talking* once in a while *and listen to God.*

Perhaps the reason so few of us have a clear perception of the work of the Holy Spirit in our lives is that we too seldom relax our thinking so as to hear God. If we are preoccupied with our "beta" belief structure, there is little room for the Holy Spirit to bring new insight into our conscious minds. To put it another way, if we do not periodically relax our preconceived notion of what is possible, how can new possibilities emerge? Coleridge called it the "willing suspension of disbelief."

There are a wide variety of ways to relax the mind/body/spirit. In the meditative prayers that follow in chapter 13, we will experience some of those ways as a preparation for prayer. However, I encourage you to explore additional methods of relaxing in order to find the ones that work best for you. As a source of methods I particularly recommend *Relax,* edited by John White and James Fadiman.

As in the development of any skill or technique, there are challenges along the path. The goal is to relax body/mind/ spirit deeply enough so as to enter the meditative state of consciousness—*and yet remain awake.* We have a life-long habit of being tense when we are awake and in beta, and falling asleep when we enter the alpha-theta state of consciousness. That is precisely why it is important to consider this a skill-development *process,* and to practice, practice, practice. It will be quite natural in the practicing to fall asleep some of the time—as I said, we have for a long time "practiced" falling asleep when we deeply relax. You might experiment with different postures. If you are sitting up when you practice your meditative prayers and you feel that you are not getting relaxed enough, try lying down. If you have been lying down and falling asleep, try sitting up. Find the ways that best bring you to deep relaxation while remaining awake.

CONCENTRATION

In any aspect of life, if we are going to realize our full potential, concentration is a crucial skill. It is no less so in meditative prayer. Frequently in our culture we give plaudits to someone possessing this skill, yet we exist in a desert in terms of teaching tools for people to use in developing and enhancing this skill.

Athletics in America is a case in point. In the years I spent in organized athletics, I frequently heard coaches, fellow athletes, or the public and press applaud the concentration of an athlete, but never can I recall any suggestions about practicing this skill. Practice is spent only on the physical skills of sport, yet the mental skill of concentration is just as important, if not more so.

Recently my wife, Diane, and I were aboard a plane flying from San Francisco to Chicago. As we were taking our seats, I casually glanced at the seat behind me; there sat one of my childhood heroes! Outwardly I was "cool" and made no indication of anything being out of the ordinary, but little Bobby Keck down deep inside kept yelling, "Wow! There he is. I mean—there he *really* is, right there behind me—Joe DiMaggio!"

For some time (it's a long flight from San Francisco to Chicago) I had an inner dialogue between the little boy who wanted to strike up a conversation with Joe DiMaggio and the adult who saw that people were constantly asking the poor guy for autographs and he probably wanted a little rest. Bad weather prevented us from landing in Chicago, and much circling and a decision to send us to Cleveland substantially prolonged the flight. This allowed time enough for Joe DiMaggio to be finished with the autograph seekers—and for me to lower my resistance about approaching him with the question I had been turning over in my mind. Finally, I asked Joe DiMaggio if he had even seen concentration taught during his experience in professional baseball. His reply was, "Never in my born days have I heard of such a thing."

I have nevertheless continued to believe that concentration *can* be taught. What does this have to do with meditative prayer? In our meditative prayer workshops, just as in my experience in athletics, I have heard people say many times: "So and so has good concentration, but I just can't seem to do it." That kind of statement reveals what many of us still think, that is, concentration or lack of it is a congenital condition beyond our control. This is not true. You *can* learn to concentrate better if, as with any other skill, you are willing to practice it.

Concentration is really *control over attention.* In everything you do, you are practicing either having your attention under your control or being determined by every stray thought, sight, or sound that comes along. With this in mind, just decide to be more aware of where you want your attention to be, and keep it there regardless of distracting thoughts, sounds, or sights.

With only a little observation we can see how our mind is accustomed to flitting about from thought to thought and connection to connection. We may be thinking about one thing at a given moment, that triggers another thought, and in a split second our mind is off on another tangential thought, and so on until we stop to wonder how we ever got to the particular thing we are thinking about. Practicing concentration will help one gain some control over the skittering mind and allow one to focus one's attention. It is possible, through practice, to make the transition from being scatterbrained to having a finely honed control over attention.

There are three difficulties to be conquered in order to be successful at improving one's concentration. The first is tension. There has been in our culture an unfortunate subliminal association of concentration with tension. Consequently, when we try to concentrate on something, we furrow our brow, clench our teeth, tense our muscles, sometimes even unconsciously, assuming that these actions improve concentration. For the real student of concentration, this association must be unlearned. The best control over one's attention is through relaxed concentration—*attention without tension.* You can practice this simply by being aware of what is happening to you physiologically when you are controlling your attention. This is the point at which the first two techniques of meditative prayer, relaxation and concentration come into play together.

The second difficulty is overcoming distractions. Distractions can be either internal or external. For instance, it is not only noises or sights but also the mind's habit of hopping from thought to thought that interrupts an attempt at concentrating. The worst way to deal with distractions is to energize them by getting angry or discouraged. The best way to deal with them is to recognize that they are inevitable and to decide how to react. For instance, if I am trying to meditate and just as I really get into it, a siren whines its way past my house, it may be sufficiently loud to grab my attention momentarily away from my object of concentration. If I let this be simply a momentary shift of attention and I calmly regain control, returning to the object of my concentration, little or no effectiveness is lost. If, on the other hand, I react to the distraction with anger and hostility, and blame that blankety-blank siren for ruining my meditation, then the concentration is lost. It was not the siren that ruined my meditation, but my reaction to the siren.

The final difficulty I want to mention is discouragement. Most accomplishments of value take time, and developing the skill of concentration certainly is no exception. Like the development of any other major skill, it will take time, patience, and perseverance. I would also like to suggest that, just as you would in the development of any skill, you should provide yourself with exercises of increasing degrees of difficulty. You might want to start practicing concentration in an environment relatively free of any visual or aural distractions, finding a quiet room, a quiet time of day, and closing your eyes to concentrate. You also might want to start with a relatively short period of time in which you attempt to control your attention. Increasingly, however, incorporate a greater degree of difficulty in your exercises. For instance, practice control of attention when there are sounds that could be distracting. Practice concentration with your eyes open so that there are visual distractions, and increase the amount of time during which you try to control your attention.

One of the more difficult exercises and one to begin to work up to is provided by the "commercial break" on your TV set. While watching television, without altering the visual or aural bombardment coming from the set, select an object in the room just slightly past the set in your line of vision to the screen. When the commercial comes on, you have a minute or two in which to practice concentration with plenty of challenging distractions. Practice under these circumstances keeping your attention relaxed and focused on some thought or object separate from all the distractions in that environment.

A simpler exercise with which you might want to start is to place a pencil in front of you and spend a few moments trying to keep your attention focused only on the pencil. Ignore distracting thoughts, sights, or sounds by gently bringing your attention back to the pencil, without irritation. Your mind is accustomed to constant movement, so it will be difficult at first to accomplish perfect stillness of attention. Consequently, you may want to begin by allowing some movement of thought within the context of the pencil. For instance, let your attention be on the color or colors in the pencil and then consider the texture of the pencil (not actually picking it up but simply thinking about the feel of it), and so on through various properties of the pencil.

Sometimes it is even entertaining to let your imagination move onto such matters as: What would it be like to be very small and try to climb over the pencil? or, If the graphite were absent, what would it be like to crawl through the center channel? To make these practice sessions more and more difficult: (1) extend the time you keep your attention focused on the pencil, and (2) narrow your focus even further (e.g., consider only the eraser). You might find it more meaningful to select a painting or symbol to use for concentration exercises. The difficulty then, however, is keeping your mind from wandering onto related thoughts.

Be kind to yourself and allow a process of growth. As you begin some of these exercises, you will become aware of how surreptitiously the mind slips in other thoughts. As with any skill, you should not expect to be accomplished at it the moment you start. And you should expect to practice, practice, and practice in order to realize results. You will find your mind responding to these exercises for developing concentration. You may also become aware of your natural moments of concentration, noticing that when you are happy or very interested in something, petty annoyances go almost unfelt. This is the state of mind you are training yourself to reproduce whenever you wish. And as you begin to master the art of concentration, you will find that all dimensions of life hold increased treasure. Our minds are exciting, mysterious instruments, great and wonderful gifts indeed.

IMAGERY

We have already examined the value of imagery in an altered state of consciousness. Now, how do we improve the skill of thinking in images rather than in words?

Try this: Close your eyes, take a couple of deep breaths, and relax. Now imagine a table in front of you with many different types of fruit on it. See the apples, oranges, grapes, watermelons, and bananas. Imagine now that you are picking up an apple in your left hand and a grape in your right hand. Now, be aware of the difference in weight. Feel it in your muscles. Put the grape down, and with both hands, let your fingers roam over the surface of the apple, "feel" the undulations on the slick skin. "See" the color and the different shadings. Now take a bite out of the apple. How does it "taste"?

In such an exercise you can quickly discover what type of imagery comes easily for you and what type comes with more difficulty. Could you "see" the fruit on the table and the color and shape of the apple as you held it before you? Did you have difficulty "feeling" the differences in weight between the apple and the grape and "feeling" the skin of the apple, or did you find it difficult to "taste" the apple? Or was it the other way around? Are you better at kinesthetic imagery than visual imagery?

The point of this exercise is to discover what imagistic skills you need to practice. As in the development of any skill, in order to develop versatility, practice that which does not come easily for you. The method of practice is quite simple. If visual imagery is difficult for you, select an object before you; look at it and study it; then close your eyes and see how long you can hold that image in your mind's eye. As soon as it fades away, open your eyes to refresh your visual memory, then repeat the process. If kinesthetic imagery is difficult, give yourself the experience of actually feeling something, then try "feeling" it in your imagination, and so on with the various senses.

Imagery is used in meditative prayer in two ways. For some meditative prayers we *direct* the imagery, that is, we select what imagery we want to use in a particular prayer, and then direct the action using that imagery. In other meditative prayers we simply receive the imagery, letting it bubble up into conscious awareness from the rich and deep well of the personal and collective unconscious or, if you will, from the deeper ranges of the spirit. Some meditative prayers combine both uses of imagery—directing the imagery in order to get oneself into the most catalytic posture of body/mind/spirit, then becoming receptive and watching, listening, and feeling the imagery as it just happens.

It needs also to be said that one must be careful to select *positive* imagery. Imagery is powerful, whether it is positive or negative. God has given us tremendous power in the so-called external world, such as in atomic and electrical power, but that power can do harm or good, depending upon the wisdom and motivation of our stewardship. Likewise with the power of the so-called internal world, wisdom and motivation determine how the God-given power will heal or hurt. Such is the response-ability with which God has created us. Electricity can kill or give light. Concentrated imagery can heal or harm, either ourselves or others. Thus, we choose to be stewards of that power either by aligning ourselves with the love of God and focusing upon positive imagery or by participating in a form of voodoo (however sophisticated) through negative imagery.

Anyone familiar with modern psychology knows how subtle this can be. At one level we may "think" we want to be healed, yet at a deeper level we may want attention or an excuse for not striving or any number of other "rewards" that come from being ill or dying. Why is it that a number of Dr. Simonton's patients simply refuse to use the relaxation and imagery prescription that he gives them? He speculates that the reason is that they must first admit they permitted themselves to develop the cancer, and that is a difficult admission to make.

In addition to being positive, it is important that the imagery selected correspond as closely as possible with our memory and with our belief structure. The more powerfully we recall a specific feeling or mental picture, the more effective it is in engaging our total body/mind/spirit. For instance, Miriam, my secretary, for warming her hands uses the image of having her hands around a hot coffee mug. Not being a coffee drinker, that experience is not a common one for me and therefore not a strong memory.

Likewise, with belief structure, if you select an image that generates disbelief and skepticism, it will not be an effective one. Using as an image something in which you readily and strongly believe will be more powerful. For example, if your theology is oriented toward Jesus, you might find a meditative prayer visualizing Jesus as healer is very effective for you. If, on the other hand, you believe more in the modern physician when it comes to healing, then that would determine your most effective imagery.

Relaxation, concentration, and imagery—these are the techniques for you to develop if you want to avail yourself of the full potentiality in meditative prayer. These techniques can then be applied within the different types of meditative prayer.

CHAPTER 13

Types of
Meditative Prayer

There are four types, or categories, of meditative prayer, which taken together provide a well-rounded approach to Christian prayer. They are not mutually exclusive, nor need they be used separately or necessarily in the following order. These four types of prayer are: (1) communion with God simply because God is God; (2) communion with God for self-actualization; (3) communion with God in our linkage with others; and (4) communion with God in order to listen.

The following are only *examples* of meditative prayer, certainly not the only ones, nor necessarily the best ones. You, in your own creative spiritual disciplines, may use any variety of relaxation procedures and images. You may select biblical images or other images from your own life and imagination. As you are learning this style of praying through these examples, you may want to read over the printed meditative prayer and then hold it in your mind, remembering it.

Another way to use these prayers is to record them onto a cassette and then let yourself be led by your own voice. (If you are reading these meditative prayers for a tape or for someone else to follow, it is important to do so with a very relaxed, slow, and soft voice. This will correspond better with the meditative state of consciousness.) Yet another method is to have one person lead another individual or a group. The latter, of course, is the way meditative prayer can be integrated into a worship service.

The possibilities in meditative prayer in terms of style and content are limitless. We can go as far in devising prayers as the human imagination can sense our communion with God.

COMMUNION WITH GOD SIMPLY BECAUSE GOD IS GOD

It is probably the most consistent and dominant theme in Christian understanding of prayer that we pray sometimes not for what we may get out of it but simply to commune with the ground and source of life. Historically, communion with God simply because God is God has been central to the Christian concept of prayer. We find it in Jesus, Paul, Augustine, Calvin, Barth, and many others. This is prayer without an agenda—concentrated only on fellowship with the living God. In our agenda, task-oriented mentality, it does not frequently occur to us—nor is it particularly easy—to just *be*—to just be with the ground of being, to become centered with that divine center of all life.

We may agree or disagree with various theologies that have been purported throughout the history of humankind, but we all have that deep inner longing for the ultimate in meaning that comes from "being at home" spiritually. Our spirits came from God and are restless until they find that communion. It is the peace that passes understanding because it is not only an intellectual activity.

In a filmed interview with Carl Jung for the British Broadcasting Corporation, the interviewer asked Dr. Jung whether he was raised in a Christian home and whether he, as a child, believed in God. "Oh yes," Dr. Jung replied. "Do you believe in God, now?" the interviewer asked the elderly and now famous scientist-researcher of the unconscious. There was a pause; Dr. Jung seemed to have difficulty in answering the question; then with a twinkle in his eye, he said, "I know. I don't need to believe; I know!"[1]

That *knowing* of God's presence in our lives comes through an encounter deeper than intellectual and analytical thought. Dr. Jung was able to know God's presence because he meditated and paid attention to his dreams. A major void in current theological education is created because meditation and dream work are not taught as means of experiencing that knowledge. Eventually they will be, as theological schools recover this biblical theme and respond to the new image of the human being.

There are many different types of images that one could use for this kind of meditative prayer—limited only by one's imagination. One can search the Bible and other Christian literature for helpful images; one can use images of God from other religions (who also have ways of knowing the God of all humankind); one can learn from conversations with other meditators what images have been helpful; or, one can search one's *own imagination* for the images that seem best in bringing to conscious awareness the all-pervading and living presence of God.

EXAMPLE

First read Psalm 8.

Now, just allow yourself to relax very deeply, relaxing in body, mind, and spirit, allowing yourself to let go of all the stress and tension that we carry with us physiologically, psychologically, spiritually, and just trusting, trusting in the presence of God in the very depths of your being.

Because of the close interrelationship of your body, mind, and spirit, if you just think "relaxation," you will begin to move in that direction. In your consciousness, now, feel or see your feet and your ankles and feel them beginning to relax, let go—becoming very loose and limp—very, very deeply relaxed. As those muscles relax, you are just letting the stress and tension flow out, away from your body.

Now, focus your mind on the calves of your legs. Feel those muscles letting go—relaxing . . . relaxing. Now, become aware of the muscles in your thighs, letting those bigger muscles of the legs relax—becoming very loose and limp—very, very deeply relaxed. And now the muscles of your hips and groin—just allow the chair or floor to hold you up, no need to retain an excess amount of stress or tension.

And now the muscles of the stomach and abdomen. This is a place where we frequently and unconsciously hold tension, so give particular attention to it, allowing those muscles to let go—relax . . . relax. Feel your body becoming liberated from the kind of stress that you ordinarily carry around with you. And now the muscles of your lower back—letting go . . . letting go. Let that feeling of relaxation now begin to work up your back, to include the muscles of your upper back, and then around your rib cage to include the muscles of your chest.

You are very, very deeply relaxed, just allowing yourself to breathe smoothly and easily. Let your whole being become very, very deeply, deeply relaxed. And now let your consciousness focus in on your shoulders, another place where we often hold tension. Feel those muscle fibers loosening up and letting go of all the stress and the tension—becoming loose, limp. And now feel that sense of relaxation coming out to the edges of your shoulder, then down your arms—including the upper arm—gradually moving down into your forearms, out into your wrists . . . hands . . . fingers. Very, very deeply, deeply relaxed, now bring your consciousness back up to your neck—allowing those muscles to relax—

retaining only enough tension to keep your head comfortable
and getting rid of all excess tension. As that relaxation works
up the back of your neck and begins to include your scalp, goes
up over the top of your head and now into the muscles of your
forehead, linger for a moment on the muscles of your forehead
and eyes. Let those muscles relax . . . relax . . . relax. Now
down across the rest of your face—including your jaw—let go
of all excess stress and tension, and as you feel your body
relaxing, very, very deeply, feel also your letting go of
intellectual concern, emotional preoccupation. Allow yourself
totally in body, mind, and spirit to be free of stress and tension
and preoccupation. Allow yourslf to be liberated from all those
concerns for a few moments. Experience the lightness—the
freedom—of being very, very deeply relaxed and yet
mentally alert. Deeply, deeply relaxed.

Imagine that you are out on a lazy summer day, hiking along
a riverbank. From time to time you pause to study the detail
of wild flowers or of the water as it flows over rocks and tree
roots near the water's edge. Be aware of the trees, the dirt,
the rocks, the breeze. Feel very much attuned to the nature
that is all about you.

As you stroll along, you come to a very soft grassy area next
to the riverbank. Sit or lie down and just allow yourself to feel
very calm and lazy. You doze off now and then, feeling a very
relaxed sense of serenity and harmony with all the forces of
life about you. The time seems to pass—effortlessly—and
soon the darkness of night envelops you and your part of the
world. You become aware of a deep black sky filled with an
array of sparkling stars—an absolutely beautiful sight. You
feel the enormity of the universe and the vastness of God's
power and creation. You feel that all this exists in a finely
honed balance. You feel a sense of gratitude and thankfulness
for your participation in that universe.

The God who created this universe is here, present—in your life. You are related to all that you see. You are a special, unique, original creation of God. Sense the awe, the wonder. Now, pick out a star and follow the light of that star, coming to earth, right down to you there looking at it. That light enters and touches your body—moving down deep into each minute cell of your body—where there again is a universe of finely honed balance, where God's spirit is the creative and sustaining force. Let yourself bask in the sense of your uniqueness and your participation in the vastness of the universe. Experience the awe and the wonder and your special place in being at home with the God that has created all of the universe—being loved . . . being accepted . . . just as you are . . . with no need to earn God's love. Just be—for you are loved. Bask in his communion with God for a period of time. Let yourself fully experience it.

Then after a while, knowing that you can return to this spot again if you would like, begin to leave this spot, carrying with you the sense of being at home with the God of the universe, the sense of being accepted just as you are and appreciating the vastness of the universe. Carry that feeling with you as you begin gradually to let your awareness return to a surface state of consciousness—back to external, physical reality.

Gradually—at a pace that is comfortable for you—allow your consciousness to begin to rise to the surface. When you are ready to be again fully alert, take a deep breath—reenergize your body—and then blink and stretch. You will be fully alert.

COMMUNION WITH GOD FOR FULL SELF-ACTUALIZATION

A Christian concept of prayer does not start or end with oneself, but at least it does *include* oneself. Any concept of communion with God that does not include movement toward full actualization of our potential—potential for physical, mental, and spiritual health and wholeness—is too small a concept of prayer. Remember that Jesus said that the first and greatest commandment is that we love the Lord with *all* our abilities.

We have already touched upon the many kinds of ableness that can be released through the synergetic use of the body/mind/spirit. Possibilities range from aborting perception of pain, altering blood flow, increasing energy, and many other physiological challenges to dealing with fear, phobias, and addictions.

Phyllis, a participant in a meditative prayer group, tells a story about the physiological possibilities of meditative prayer. A bright, zestful, attractive woman, Phyllis is a wife and mother and a pharmacist.

In April, 1974, after forming a business which is aggressive and competitive, not only was I in debt up to my eyelids and working as the only registered pharmacist handling more bed patients than a hospital in town, but I was also pregnant. After months of struggle and working sixty-five to seventy-five hours a week at the company, with the mental strain of the business, I began to have blinding, vise-like headaches.

One morning while attending a Medicare Utilization Review Committee meeting, I had one of the most severe headaches I have had, and one of the physicians on the committee took me immediately to my obstetrician. After a thorough examination, my obstetrician advised me that the cause of the headache and perception problems I was having was the sudden development of extremely high blood pressure. He further informed me that I was a candidate for a stroke and that he wanted me to immediately quit working and stay in bed most of the day. My physician further stated that unless this hypertension was controlled, he felt there might be damage to the baby.

In spite of her extraordinarily busy life, Phyllis had become fascinated with the possibilities of meditative prayer and had become involved in some of our research. When this problem of hypertension emerged, Phyllis came to me to talk about what imagery she could use in her meditative prayers. We discussed the matter for a while, and when I suggested one possibility, namely, imagining the blood slipping and sliding through her veins without any obstruction or difficulty, her face lit up. She knew we had hit upon the imagery that would work for her. In her work she deals with Teflon-coated tubing. "That's it," she thought, "I'll visualize my veins coated with Teflon so that the blood easily moves along."

Within two months my blood pressure was lowered from 190/135 to 120/78 and remained so through natural delivery. My physician continues to comment on how happy he is for us all that my pressure lowered but remains baffled or skeptical that it could be controlled mentally.

Although I have not had any problem with elevated blood pressure for more than ten months now and my work schedule is just as rigorous, I do continue as part of my daily meditative prayer the visualization of blood cells slipping through smooth-walled veins and arteries and the gauge on the sphygmomanometer at the normal range.

This story led to another. A colleague of mine, the Reverend Bud Huntzicker, told me one day that he was caught completely by surprise when he was turned down as a blood donor because of high blood pressure (160/110). He asked me what I knew about the effectiveness of using meditative prayer to control high blood pressure, and I shared with him some of the evidence, including the story about Phyllis. Bud is not a pharmacist, but he was able to use the imagery of Teflon-coated veins very successfully. He used this imagery for three weeks, and in spite of his usual schedule of activities, pressures, and stress situations, his blood pressure was 120/60 at his next doctor's appointment. The other day I got a note from Bud that read:

> Gadzooks! Recently I again went to give blood, deliberately meditating while sitting and waiting for fifteen minutes—using the Teflon imagery. The nurse was startled when she took my blood pressure, took it again, and announced a reading of 110/68. She asked me if I were taking medicine! What really feels good is that I have gained an inner confidence that this aspect of my health is controllable.

That's precisely the feeling that more and more of us will have as we begin to fully actualize the power that God has created within us.

First, you must determine what your agenda, or challenge, is. Then search your memory for the most vivid image that accomplishes that purpose.

For an example of this type of meditative prayer, let's assume that you are faced with a general low energy level, physically, and fogginess, psychologically. If sunlight is meaningful to you, both literally and symbolically, then that may be the best image for you.

EXAMPLE

Go through a similar relaxation procedure as in the first sample meditative prayer, only this time, tense each set of muscles before relaxing them. For instance, tense the muscles of your feet and ankles, holding them tense for a few seconds, and then relax them, feeling a dramatic release of the tension. Continue this throughout the musculature of your body. Also, don't forget to relax completely your emotions and intellect.

Imagine, now, that you are walking along a secluded beach, feeling very much at peace. You have a sense of serenity and are in a vacation mood. You have under your arm either a light lawn chair, if that is what you like to sit in at the beach, or a blanket that you can lie on. As you walk along the beach, select a place where you will be comfortable sitting or lying down. Settle down at that spot and just relax, experiencing the beauty of the scene and feeling a part of nature. And as you sit or lie back, feel the warmth of the sun on your face. Be aware of the clear blue sky, a few white fluffy clouds here and there, some birds flitting past, the beauty of the water there before you, and the warmth of the fine-grained sand.

It's a very comfortable and relaxing beautiful scene. Be aware of how you are a part of the whole scheme of nature so that in a very real way you participate in all the reality about you. God has created you, has created all that surrounds you, all of which is intertwined, interlinked in all the energy systems of the universe.

Focus your attention now on the sensation of the sun on your face. As you tilt your head back, you experience the warmth of those sun rays. The air is cool and crisp, and you have a very comfortable feeling of the warmth of the sun bathing your face. Let your imagination now begin to focus on the realization that the sun is the energy source for our solar system. It is from the sun, directly or indirectly, that we get all our energy, all our life, and you are sitting there, now able to absorb that very energy, coming directly from the sun into the very cells of your body. Let yourself experience that.

While you feel the sun's rays entering your skin, bringing energy to each and every cell of your body, also let your mind wander over the realization that the sun, spelled *s-o-n,* said, "I am the light of the world." Experience that light as it enlightens every dimension of your body, mind, and spirit. Experience that energy as it energizes every dimension of your body—and spirit. Let yourself relax and absorb that freely given light and energy. You don't have to earn it—God gives it to you freely—just receive, feel the process of absorption taking place, light going to every nook and cranny of your mind, the energy moving into every dimension of your being. As you sit there absorbing that light—that sun—the energy and the enlightenment from God—feel it having an effect upon your very being, every dimension of your being.

Linger for as long as you like, experiencing the warming, energizing, and enlightening effects of the sun, and the Son. When you feel you have received all that you are able to absorb at this time, and knowing that you can return again, prepare to leave. But before you leave that scene, pause for a moment, again being aware of the sand, the water, the sky, and feel a deep sense of gratitude, thankfulness, for the fact that you can participate with God in all of creation.

With a new sense of enlightenment and energy and with this powerful sense of gratitude and thankfulness, now prepare to go. Pick up your blanket or chair and begin moving back down the beach. As you walk down the beach be aware that you feel more energized. You feel more centered. You now carry light and energy in every cell of your body. As you walk further down the beach, gradually that scene begins to fade, and you begin to become more aware of where you were physically before this meditative prayer.

At a pace that is comfortable for you, let yourself make the transition from the beach back to where you physically are now, returning gradually to a surface state of consciouness but carrying with you the benefits of your meditative prayer and your sense of gratitude. When you are ready to be fully alert, simply decide to be so. Take a deep breath, blink, stretch, and be fully alert.

COMMUNION WITH GOD
IN OUR LINKAGE WITH OTHERS

Any concept of prayer if it is to be Christian must include love, concern, and involvement for and with other people. Traditionally this concern has been expressed in intercessory prayer, whether a verbal prayer or a social-action prayer. An act of social justice obviously implies love for our fellow brothers and sisters. Verbal, or meditative, praying for someone else, however, is having a hard time these days in terms of credibility. Many people think praying for someone else may make the prayer feel better—one has at least tried—but it's rather difficult to believe that it actually does the one being prayed for any good. This credibility problem may be the result of (1) a "satellite" image of God, which is crumbling, and (2) the feeling that we are basically isolated and insulated beings: How could my thoughts have any effect on someone miles away?

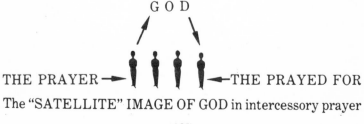

The "SATELLITE" IMAGE OF GOD in intercessory prayer

This illustration offers a visual representation of what I am talking about. Many people have believed in a God who was "up there" or "out there" and to whom we prayed, asking that God do something for so-and-so. God would then send the favor down to the other person. This picture also represents how we often feel we are distinctly separate, unrelated beings—there are no visible connections.

Intercessory prayer has lost its credibility for many as the image of God being "up there" or "out there" has begun to crumble and the image of isolated human beings remains. Consequently, all that seems to be left is a belief in direct verbal or active communication. If I can tell or show the other person I care for him or her, that is effective. But praying for someone in another city, how does that do any good?

Part of the problem is that we continue to observe reality primarily with beta consciousness, the type of consciousness that perceives *distinctions* and *separation*. If, however, we move deeper, into the type of consciousness that perceives our *linkages* and *interrelationships,* the picture looks like this.

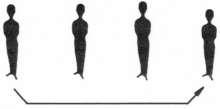

GOD

When we get into these deeper states of consciousness, we perceive and experience the profound ways that we are all interrelated. My friends who are careful theologians warn me against implying that God is *only* in our depths. They are right, and I do not mean to imply that. What I am suggesting is that beta consciousness tends to emphasize our separateness, and altered states of consciousness seem to enable us to have a more profound experience of the oneness of all.

There is ample scientific verification for this perception. Carl Jung, who analyzed literally thousands of dreams and meditations, said that in the depths of the unconscious, "man is no longer a distinct individual, but his mind widens out and merges into the mind of mankind—not the conscious mind, but the unconscious mind of mankind, where we are all the same."[2] It is more recent research, however, that may provide the most dramatic indication of our interrelatedness.

Two physicists at the prestigious Stanford Research Institute, Harold Puthoff and Russell Targ, have been conducting research on what they are calling "remote vision." What is remarkable about the results of these experiments is that they indicate that "ordinary" people can perform in ways formerly attributed only to "psychics."

Here is how the experiment works. Suppose you were the subject for this particular test. Dr. Targ would ask you to relax very deeply and to concentrate on where Dr. Puthoff is at that moment. You are not supposed to know where he is. Actually, Dr. Puthoff is off some distance—perhaps out of the city, or even out of the country—taking photographs of his environment, knowing that at that specified time, you, the subject, will be trying to describe his environment. Dr. Targ tells you to relax, concentrate, and wait for an image to appear. When it does, describe it and/or draw it. Later, a panel of scientists will see whether your description and Dr. Puthoff's photographs match. In tests like this, the correlation has been so high that Dr. Targ has said, "We are proving unequivocally that there is a paranormal channel of human communication. We don't know how it works, but it works reliably and independent of distances."[3]

Telepathy research also points to the linkages we all share. The fact that this research seems to be discovering something about *how* these communication channels work is helpful to those of us who want to enhance these abilities in intercessory prayer.

The Russians have been involved in telepathic research extensively for some time. In addition to the usual tests of *mental* telepathy, the Russians have monitored physiological responses. Among their most significant discoveries are (1) people can be trained to be successful at telepathy; (2) particularly good telepathic communication can take place between people who have biological compatibility, or what the Russians call "bio-rapport," such as that between parent and child; (3) emotion, particularly strong emotion, seems to be the most easily recieved kind of "message"; (4) distances make no difference in telepathic sending and receiving (telepathy can be as successful from thousands of miles away as it is from the next room); (5) persons pick up messages aimed at them telepathically with their bodies as well as with their conscious minds. Even if the conscious mind does not pick up the message, there is a physiological response to the message. Physical pain and discomfort can be transmitted, so why not healing, joy, comfort, and love? The fact that our bodies can pick up telepathic messages would seem to be convincing evidence that even a person in a coma can receive and benefit from our intercessory prayers.

Sheila Ostrander and Lynn Schroeder, authors of *Psychic Discoveries Behind the Iron Curtain* and *A Handbook of PSI Discoveries,* have done a considerable amount of investigation on telepathy and other psychic phenomena. They have compiled a list of the techniques for sending and receiving telepathy from the results of various researchers.

How to send a message telepathically—
Relax physically and mentally. Feel sure of success.
Concentrate and saturate yourself with the target image.
Chant the image of the target silently to yourself.
Send pulsing images to a definite destination, the mind of
    your receiver. Release each image; send them out on
    the mental waves one after another.

How to receive a message telepathically—
Relax and don't try too hard.
Visualize a blank screen in your mind. Look for the image
    to appear. Command your unconscious mind, Give me
    the answer now. A sort of uncaring alertness works
    best.
Wait for an image to form. Don't guess.
Differentiate, try to notice cues that indicate the
    difference between the right and wrong image. Often
    incorrect pictures flicker and dissolve.

I do have a disagreement with Ostrander and Schroeder's list even though it means I am challenging the "pros." There are far too many cases of telepathic messages being sent and received while in a crisis to accept without question that relaxation is a necessary condition. It seems rather, that concentration is the key factor. In a crisis a person's mind is concentrated on the problem at hand so powerfully that unintentional telepathic communication can take place. In meditative prayer one's concentration is enhanced by deep relaxation.

I had the experience of receiving such a message during a meditative prayer early in my research. I was in Midland, Texas, conducting a workshop in meditative prayer. During an afternoon break, I was spending some time in prayer. I was trying simply to be receptive regarding the people and the process of the workshop. To my surprise, a clear image of my daughter, Lindsay, popped into my consciousness. It was a visual image—as clear as a photograph. Since I had not "directed" or chosen that imagery, I felt there was some reason why it had occurred—a reason, however, unknown to my conscious mind.

Feeling that the imagery was significant, I went immediately to the telephone to call home. Logically it did not make sense that Lindsay would be at home; it was Monday afternoon during school hours. Nevertheless, it was Lindsay who answered the telephone. She was excited, shrieking, traumatized, and effusive. (Anyone with a thirteen-year-old daughter can appreciate the scene.) When she calmed down, she explained to me that earlier in the day she had been injured in a school athletic contest, had spent part of the day in the emergency room at the hospital, was in a great deal of discomfort, *and was wishing very strongly that her daddy would call.* When she answered the telephone to hear me on the other end, the "coincidence" blew her mind—and mine too! (Oh, thou of little faith!)

My experience and the research I have cited simply illustrate the considerable evidence that God has created us with a profound interrelationship. Intercessory prayer makes sense, and we can learn from a variety of research *how* we can improve our stewardship of this ability.

Matt. 25:34-45 expresses this interrelatedness very vividly for the Christian. Jesus points out here that all life is so interrelated that if we turn our back on a brother or sister in need, we turn our back on Him. Those who asked the Son of man, from the outlook of beta consciousness, "Lord, when did we see thee hungry or thirsty or a stranger or naked or sick or in prison, and did not minister to thee?" were told, "As you did it not to one of the least of these, you did it not to me." Jesus

It is interesting how that symbolism carried over into other meditative prayers for Rick. He reports that a short time later he was in a receptive meditative prayer, asking God for some guidance on a particular problem. He waited, and then, in his own words, "Suddenly there is a light surrounding me that turns into a light bulb. The light bulb is above me. It is very large and I feel the warmth of the light. To my surprise, the light bulb becomes an air balloon and carries me upward. As I ascend into the air, I get a broader view of my problems—I see them in a new light!"

It would seem that God speaks to us primarily through symbols because it is a more holistic way of communicating—it engages *all* the dimensions of our being, not just the intellect. Consequently, we are seriously limited in our ability to grasp the fullness of spiritual experience if we can only speak and hear the language of the literal word—the language of the intellect, of beta consciousness.

This helps explain why Jesus always taught in parables. When describing the kingdom of God, he does not give us a literal description because the kingdom of God is a much more profound reality. No, he gives imagistic and symbolic descriptions.

The kingdom of heaven may be compared to a man who sowed good seed in his field. (Matt. 13:24)

The kingdom of heaven is like a mustard seed. . . . (Matt. 13:31)

The kingdom of heaven is like the yeast a woman took and mixed in with three measures of flour till it was leavened all through. (Matt. 13:33 JB)

In all this Jesus spoke to the crowds in parables; indeed, he would never speak to them except in parables. (Matt. 13: 34-35 JB)

That is all very frustrating to us. Why doesn't Jesus explain things more concretely? But like it or not, this seems to be the primary language of spiritual reality. When we learn to speak and hear this language, we begin to see how it indeed is a more holistic language, speaking to all levels of our being.

Even before being concerned about interpreting the messages, however, we need to learn how to prepare ourselves to receive them. One possibility is the complete free-lance "trip." That is done simply by relaxing very deeply and then waiting for the imagery to bubble up into conscious awareness. For most of us, though, it is easier to set the stage and use certain catalytic images to aid our receptivity. For instance, you could use the image of going to an art gallery to pick up a painting that has been done just for you. When you unwrap it, don't *determine* what will appear but *wait* for whatever will appear on the canvas. Whatever appears carries a message for you.

It is not just coincidence, for instance, that I frequently find myself in meditative prayers driving a car that is out of control just at the times in my life when God is telling me to slow down.

Some meditative disciplines suggest that the images that bubble up into conscious awareness are superfluous, unimportant. I disagree! God is working for your health and wholeness and is giving you plenty of clues—if you will listen. Drawing upon the biblical literature as well as Jungian psychology and creativity literature, the philosophy behind meditative prayer holds that the images coming forth during a receptive time carry symbolic messages that can be used for problem solving.

This is not to say that all the imagery will be pleasant. Pleasant or scary, happy or sad, the images can be used for insight, growth, and transformation. God may, in other words, let you experience the agony of a death before the glory of a resurrection.

Meditative prayer of the receptive type can also be used to enrich Bible study. Traditionally, Bible study is approached in the beta state of consciousness, with an analytic frame of mind. It should not be startling to suggest, however, that not all spiritual meaning in the Scriptures will be appropriated with the intellect and only one portion of the consciousness spectrum. Over the past three years, thousands of Christians have tried this approach, and many remarkable experiences and enthusiastic expressions have come out of this "new" kind of Bible study.

Whether you use biblical images or the catalytic images of your own mind, receptive meditative prayer holds enormous potential for you. Try the following meditative prayer.

EXAMPLE

Relax deeply by whatever method you are finding works best for you. You might try some kind of exercise prior to meditation. Once you are very deeply relaxed, imagine you are standing on a small hill overlooking a forest. Be aware of all the details of that scene, the grass, the sky, the forest, the colors, the warmth of the sun. Walk down the hill toward the forest, entering the forest by a path that is before you. Walk leisurely down the path being aware of all the minute details of the forest.

Eventually you approach a small clearing where there is a bench bathed in sunlight. On the back of the bench is the word "Exodus." Sit down on the bench, knowing that it will be a place for you to discover what is in your life now that needs to be left behind in order to experience a creative new life with God. *Be still and know.* Wait, patiently, for images to occur. Do not force or *make* images.

After a while, get up from the bench and continue on down the path. In a little while you come to a big clearing with a cottage. As you approach the cottage anticipate that there will be significant insight for you inside. Be aware of the condition of the cottage—what it looks like. When you enter the cottage, pause to observe the rooms, the furnishings, et cetera. Now, go to the back room where there is an easy chair for you to sit down in. As you sit in the chair, notice that there is a painting on the wall across from you. Pause to let emerge on that painting whatever will. *Be still and know.*

If it feels all right, enter the painting, become a part of it, experience it. After a while, step back out of the painting, return to the chair. Beside you, notice a small seed on the table. Pick up the seed, knowing that it represents a part of you waiting to blossom, wanting to grow. Take the seed to the garden outside, plant it, and wait to see what grows. *Be still and know.*

When you are ready, leave the cottage, going back through the forest and using the climbing of the hill to regain a surface state of consciousness.

Afterword

The story of meditative prayer is not complete. This is just a beginning. Everything touched on here opens doors to many other insights and experiences. There are vast new horizons to explore and new levels of love and relationship to experience—the journey goes on! And serendipity? Serendipity will always be around the corner in our journey with the Architect of life if we learn to "catch the joy as it flies."

The spirit of synergy will continue moving us into a larger image of the human being—a larger image of ourselves, our relationships with others, and our relationship with that loving and creative source of all life we call God. As we resonate with this spirit there are two hopes that I share with you in concluding this book.

One hope is that we will increase our abilities to fly high and dream big. Richard Bach reminds us that "the seagull that flies the highest sees the furthest." God's creation is so expansive and magnificent that we need not worry about reaching or transcending the limits. Our concern should be that our experience will be limited by shackled imaginations, shackled by the current boundaries and orthodoxy of medicine, psychology, and religion.

My other hope is for humility. We human journeyers have frequently demonstrated the tendency to assume that our insights and experiences must necessarily be the best for others or that the theology that is meaningful for me is the best for my neighbor or that what currently lies outside the boundaries of my belief and experience cannot be "true." The humility I am hoping for is that which comes from experiencing the wonder of God's very personal and unique relationship with each creature. Then we can celebrate and share our own experience, celebrate and learn from others' experience, and still know that God's versatility is not exhausted.

Notes

PART I

Chapter 2

1. For more information on Edgar Cayce, contact the Association for Research and Enlightenment, Inc., 67th St. at Atlantic Ave., Box 595, Virginia Beach, VA 23451.
2. For the story of Arigó I am indebted to the account by Henry K. Puharich, M.D., in *Psychic Exploration: A Challenge for Science,* ed. Edgar D. Mitchell (New York: Putnam, 1974), pp. 333-47.
3. *Ibid.,* p. 336.
4. Barbara Brown, *New Mind, New Body* (New York: Harper, 1974), p. 395.
5. Ainslie Meares, *A System of Medical Hypnosis* (New York: Julian Press, 1960), p. 50.

Chapter 3

1. One of the earliest holistic pain clinics is that set up by Dr. C. Norman Shealy, the Pain and Health Rehabilitation Center, Route 2, LaCrosse, WI 54601.

Spirit of Synergy: God's Power and You

PART II

Chapter 5

1. O. Carl Simonton and Stephanie Matthews-Simonton, "Belief Systems and Management of Emotional Aspects of Malignancy," *The Journal of Transpersonal Psychology,* 1975, no. 1, p. 38.
2. George B. Leonard, *The Transformation* (New York: Delacorte, 1960), p. 93.
3. Interview with Lewis Thomas, "Dark Secret of Doctors: Most Things Get Better by Themselves," ed. L. Edson, *New York Times Magazine,* July 4, 1976, pp. 108-9.
4. *Ibid.*
5. *Ibid.*
6. Norman Cousins, "Anatomy of an Illness (As Perceived by the Patient)," *New England Journal of Medicine,* December 23, 1976, pp. 1458-63.
7. Harvey G. Cox, *On Not Leaving It to the Snake* (New York: Macmillan, 1964), p. ix.

Chapter 6

1. Buckminster Fuller, as quoted by Marilyn Ferguson, ed., *Brain/Mind Bulletin,* June 20, 1977. For much in the concept of synergy, I am indebted to Buckminster Fuller, scientist, architect, engineer, and one of the most innovative minds of our time.
2. Pierre Teilhard de Chardin, *A Phenomenon of Man* (New York: Harper & Bros., 1959).
3. Joseph Campbell, *The Masks of God: Creative Mythology* (New York: Viking, 1961).
4. Fritjof Capra, *The Tao of Physics* (Berkeley, CA: Shambala Publications, 1975), p. 131.
5. Paolo Soleri, *The Bridge Between Matter and Spirit is Matter Becoming Spirit* (New York: Anchor Books, 1973), pp. 124-25.
6. D. R. G. Owen, *Body and Soul: A Study of the Christian View of Man* (Philadelphia: Westminster, 1956), p. 196.

Chapter 7

1. Jerome Frank, *Persuasion and Healing: A Comparative Study of Psychotherapy* (New York: Schocken Books, 1974), p. 140.
2. *Ibid.,* p. 138.

Notes

3. Thomas Chalmers, interview on tape (New York: Bio-Monitoring Applications, Inc., 1976).
4. O. Carl Simonton and Stephanie Matthews-Simonton, "Belief Systems and Management of Emotional Aspects of Malignancy," *Journal of Transpersonal Psychology*, 1975, no. 1, p. 29. For an excellent survey of this literature, see *Stress, Psychological Factors and Cancer* (Ft. Worth, TX: New Medicine Press, 1976).
5. *Ibid.*, p. 32.
6. Carlos Castanada, as quoted in Sam Keen, *Voices and Visions* (New York: Harper & Row, 1974), pp. 112-13.

Chapter 8

1. Don Gerrard, as quoted in Mike Samuels and Nancy Samuels, *Seeing with the Mind's Eye* (New York: Random House, 1975), p. xi.
2. Samuels and Samuels, *Seeing with the Mind's Eye*, p. 216.
3. Paracelsus, as quoted in *Ibid.*, p. 112.
4. O. Carl Simonton and Stephanie Matthews-Simonton, "Belief Systems and Management of Emotional Aspects of Malignancy," *Journal of Transpersonal Psychology*, 1975, no. 1, p. 33.
5. O. Carl Simonton as quoted in J. Bolen, "Meditation and Psychotherapy in the Treatment of Cancer," *Psychic Magazine*, July 1973, p. 20.
6. S. Freud, *The Ego and the Id* (New York: W. W. Norton, 1960), p. 19.
7. Sallie TeSelle, "Parable, Metaphor, and Theology," *Journal of the American Academy of Religion*, 42:631.
8. Jim Colbert in *Golf Magazine*, June 1975.
9. Jean Houston, "Putting the First Man on Earth," in *Saturday Review*, February 22, 1975, p. 32.

Chaper 9

1. My story is a modern adaptation of a Sufi story about a man looking for a key out in the street rather than in his house where he lost it because the light is better.
2. Charles Panati, *Super Senses* (New York: Quadrangle, 1974), p. 254.
3. William James, *Varieties of Religious Experience* (New York: Collier, 1961), p. 299.
4. Charles Lindbergh, *The Spirit of St. Louis* (New York: Scribner's, 1953), pp. 389-90.
5. John Brodie, in interview by Michael Murphy for *Intellectual Digest*, January 1973, as quoted in George Leonard, *The Ultimate Athlete* (New York: Viking, 1974), pp. 34-35.

Spirit of Synergy: God's Power and You

PART III

Chapter 10

1. Willis Harman, *An Incomplete Guide to the Future* (Stanford, CA: The Portable Stanford Series, 1976), p. 7.

Chapter 11

1. Summaries of the reports are available from New Wineskins Center, 1320 Cambridge Blvd., Columbus, OH 43212.

Chapter 12

1. W. Timothy Gallwey, *The Inner Game of Tennis* (New York: Random House, 1974), pp. 33, 89.
2. Ernest Wood, *Concentration: An Approach to Meditation* [1949] (Wheaton, IL: Theosophical Publishing House, A Quest Book, 1967), p. 13.

Chapter 13

1. Carl Jung, in "The Carl Jung Story" (A van der Post Film, available from the Analytical Psychology Club of Chicago).
2. Carl Jung, *Analytical Psychology: Its Theory and Practice* (New York: Pantheon Books, 1968), p. 46.
3. Dr. Russell Targ, in interview by Bruce Keidan, reported in Knight Newspapers.

Recommended Reading

The literature of the various fields discussed in this book is extensive. This list is intended as a suggested starting place for the reader interested in exploring these subjects more fully. Readers interested in workshops in meditative prayer, biofeedback, or dreams may contact: New Wineskins Center for Research and Development; 1320 Cambridge Blvd.; Columbus, OH 43212.

Christian Meditation

Johnston, William. *Silent Music: The Science of Meditation.* New York: Harper & Row, 1974.

Kelsey, Morton. *The Other Side of Silence.* New York: Paulist Press, 1976.

Pipkin, H. Wayne. *Christian Meditation: Its Art and Practice.* New York: Hawthorn, 1977.

Stahl, Carolyn. *Opening to God: Guided Imagery and Meditation on Scripture.* Nashville, TN: The Upper Room, 1977.

Holistic Healing

Pelletier, Kenneth B. *Mind as Healer, Mind as Slayer.* New York: Delacorte Press, 1977.

Sanford, John A. *Healing and Wholeness.* New York: Paulist Press, 1977.

Shealy, C. Norman. *90 Days to Self-Health.* New York: Dial Press, 1976.

Biofeedback

Brown, Barbara R. *New Mind, New Body.* New York: Harper & Row, 1974.

Green, Elmer and Alyce. *Beyond Biofeedback.* New York: Delacorte Press, 1977.

Medical Hypnosis

Fromm, Erika, and Shor, Ronald E. *Hypnosis: Research Developments and Perspectives.* Chicago: Aldine, 1972.

Meares, Ainslie. *A System of Medical Hypnosis.* New York: Julian Press, 1960.

Psychic Research

Mitchell, Edgar D. *Psychic Exploration: A Challenge for Science.* New York: Putnam's, 1974.

Ostrander, Sheila, and Schroeder, Lynn. *Psychic Discoveries Behind the Iron Curtain.* Englewood Cliffs, N.J.: Prentice-Hall, 1970.

Panati, Charles. *Super Senses.* New York: Quadrangle, 1974.

The Study of Consciousness

Brain/Mind Bulletin. Los Angeles, CA: Interface Press.

Ornstein, Robert E. *The Psychology of Consciousness.* New York: Viking Press, 1972.

Pearce, Joseph Chilton. *The Crack in the Cosmic Egg.* New York: Pocketbooks, 1973.

_____. *Exploring the Crack in the Cosmic Egg.* New York: Julian Press, 1974.

Relaxation

White, John, and Fadiman, James. *Relax.* New York: Dell, 1976.

Recommended Reading

Concentration

Gallwey, Timothy. *The Inner Game of Tennis.* New York: Random House, 1974.

Imagery

Samuels, Mike, and Samuels, Nancy. *Seeing with the Mind's Eye: The History, Techniques and Uses of Visualization.* New York: Random House, 1975.

Dreams

Faraday, Ann. *The Dream Game.* New York: Harper & Row, 1974.

Sanford, John. *Dreams: God's Forgotten Language.* Philadelphia: Lippincott, 1968.